Interesting Sayings &
Argumentative Quotes
Plus Spiritual Sayings
and
Quotes
of the Bible

Interesting Sayings &
Argumentative Quotes
Plus Spiritual Sayings
and
Quotes
of the Bible

KENNETH RUFF

ARPress
ILLUMINATING IDEAS,
EMPOWERING VOICES

ARPress
45 Dan Road Suite 5
Canton MA 02021

Hotline: 1(800) 220-7660
Fax: 1(855) 752-6001

Ordering Information:
Quantity sales. Special discounts are available on quantity purchases by corporations, associations, and others. For details, contact the publisher at the address above.

Printed in the United States of America.

ISBN-13:	Softcover	979-8-89356-269-9
	eBook	979-8-89356-267-5

Library of Congress Control Number: 2024903379

Interesting Sayings and Argumentative Quotes
written by Kenn Ruff

June 1, 2014

Due to further research, I've found more Interesting Saying and Quotes. I have revised this book from my prior finding.

I hope they are as entertaining as the first book. Enjoy!

June 4, 2016

Numbers #'s

1 bad apple spoils the whole bunch.
1 day at a time.
1 is the loneliest number.
18 karat.
2 for one.
2 is a company, and 3 is a crowd.
2 out-of-three.
2 wrongs don't make a right.
24 karat.
3 for one.
3 of a kind.
3 strikes, you're out.
3 times a lady.
3 times the charm.
4 Aces.
4 BLOOD MOONS, Joel 2, Acts 2:19-21.

4 sho!
5 and 10. (Dime)
5-0. (Police)
6 pack.
66. (Route)
666. (Mark of the beast)
7 comes eleven.
80 proof.
9 lives.
9 to 5.
10 karat.
10-4 good buddy.
14 Karat.
15 minutes of fame.
24/7.
50-50.
52 cards in a deck.
52 pickup.
52 pickup sticks.
99 and a 1/2 won't do.
99 bottles of beer on the wall.
100 proof.
1,000,000 man march.
1% of something is better than 100% of nothing.
15% of people Tithe and 85% are tippers.
70% of success in life is showing up.

"A"

A back-handed compliment.

A bad gambler never knows when to quit.

A basket case.

A bird in the hand is worth two in the bush. (Mother)

A blind squirrel finds a nut every now and then.

A blow job. (Oral sex)

A bluff is a white lie.

About as welcome as a turd in a swimming pool.

Above suspicion.

Above the law.

Above your pay grade.

A brainstorm.

A broken clock keeps the correct time twice a day.

A broke man can't gamble.

Absence makes the heart grow funder.

A bullet has no eyes.

A can of whip ass.

A catch 22.

A chain is only as strong as its weakest link, and life is after a chain.

A change is gonna come.

A chicken in every pot.

A chip off the old block.

A closed mouth never gets feed.

A crash and burn.

Action speaks louder than words.

A cut above.

A day late and a dollar short.

Add injury to insult.

A den of thieves.

A diamond in the rough.

A do-gooder.

A double-headed-sword.

A drowning man will grab at straws.

A duck out of water.

Adversity: It's not what you do when it happens but what you do after it happens.

Affairs of the heart make us all a little crazy.

A figment of your imagination.

A fish out of water.

A flare for the dramatic.

A flower is only as good as its peddles.

A fly on the wall.

A fool and his money are soon parted.

A fool chatters while a wise man listens.

A fool flatters himself, a wise man flatters the fool.

A force of habit.

Age before beauty.

A good Indian is a dead Indian.

A good King knows when to show mercy.

A good laugh is sunshine in the house.

A good woman is hard to find.

Agree to disagree.

A hard head makes a soft butt.(Mother)

A hard pill to swallow.

A hard row to hoe.

A hell of your own making.

A horned toad can tell you which way to go.

A hostile takeover.

Ain't got a pot to pess in or a window to throw it out of.

Ain't hitting a lick at a snake. (Mother)

Ain't no fun when the rabbit has the gun.

Ain't nothing to it but to do it.

Ain't worth the powder that pushes the shell.

Ain't worth two dead flies, mashed.

A jealous man can't work.

A job takes only as long as it has to.

A Killjoy.

A Kodac moment.

A lawyer who represents himself has a fool for a client.

A leopard can't change his spots.

A lesson learned.

Alfa male.

A liar should have a good memory.

A lie ain't nothing to tell.

A lie rolls downhill.

A little somein somein.

Alive and kicking.

All closed eyes aren't sleeping.

All-right.

All eyes on me.

All eyes on the prize.

All good-byes aren't gone.

All good things must come to an end.

All good things come to those who wait.

All great men have humble beginnings.

All in a day's work.

All is fair in love and war.

All men are born truthful and die, liars.
All that glitters ain't gold.
All work and no play make Jack a dull boy.
All's fair in love and war.
All's well that ends well.
All your ducks in a row.
Almighty dollar.
A low blow.
Always expect the unexpected.
Always look before you leap.
Always turn a negative situation into a positive situation.
Always wear clean underwear.
A man ain't always what he seems.
A man ain't supposed to cry.
A man begins cutting his wisdom teeth the first time he bites off more than he can chew.
A man can't throw his pride out the window.
A man is like a rope, lonely strong as it's the thinnest strand.
A man is only as big as his dreams.
A man is wealthy when he enjoys what he has.
A man never gets used to hard knocks.
A man's home is his castle.
A man's innocent until proven guilty.
A man who sticks his head in the sand, make a mighty big target.
A man who won't fight a prairie fire because it's too far away, will soon feel the heat.
A mask hides the face but frees the soul, a mask is not the truth.

A means to an end.

A menace to society.

America the beautiful.

A Mickey Fynn. (Drugged or Poisoned)

A mother's love.

An aim in life is the only fortune worth finding.

An apple a day keeps the doctor away.

An apple doesn't fall too far from the tree.

An ass kisser.

An early bird catches the worm.

A need-to-know basis.

A negative nancy.

An empty wagon makes the most noise.

Anger is an emotion.

Anger is fear on the way out.

Anger is your enemy.

An idol mine is the DEVIL's workshop.

An innocent man doesn't run.

A nose-down attitude.

A nose-up attitude.

Another day at the office.

Another one bites the dust.

Any landing that you can walk away from is a good landing.

An old fashion ass whipping.

Anything good is never easy.

Anything worth having is worth paying for and waiting for.

A one legget man in an ass kicking contest.

A one-night affair.

A pain in the ass.

A patriot should always be ready to defend his Nation, (country), against its Government.

A penny for your thoughts.

A person will sometimes devote all his life to the development of one part of his body - the Wishbone.

A picture is worth a thousand words.

A picture of a portrait isn't painted with a single color.

A piece of the rock.

A pig in a poke.

A pint to a pound makes the world go round.

A place to sleep and some food for your beak.

A poem begins in delight and ends in wisdom.

A poet and don't know it.

Apples and oranges.

Apples don't fall too far from the tree.

A preacher recognizes a Pimp.

A ready-made family.

A rebel without a cause.

Are you fucking kidding me?

A rolling stone gathers no moss.

A room without books is like a body without a soul.

A rose by any other name is still a rose.

Arrival is the end of a journey.

ASAP.

As close as one is to two.

As different as night and day.

A second-story man.

A self-made man.

A sentimental journey.

As fresh as salt.

As good as it gets.

As guilty as Cain.

As sharp as a mosquito's peter.

A shoulder to cry on.

A slap on the wrist.

As long as I owe you, you'll never go broke.

As long as one person remembers you, it isn't over.

A smoking gun.

As much is given, much is required.

As real as it gets.

As scarce as hen's teeth.

As slow as a banker agreeing to a cash loan.

A smile is just a frown turned up-side-down.

A son of a gun.

Ass out of luck. (A.O.L.)

As sure as night turns to day.

As tight as dick's hatband.

A stitch in time saves nine.

A streak of fat, a streak of lean, a streak of good, a streak of the mean.

As worthless as a four-card flush.

A teaspoon of sugar will catch more flies than a pound of vinegar.

At first, you don't succeed try, try, again.

A thing of beauty is a joy forever.

A tough nut to crack.

A tough row to hoe.

Atta boy.

At the end of the day.

*Attitudes are like flat tires, we won't get anywhere till we
change it.*

*A victory ain't nothing but the clearing of a battlefield so
another one can begin.*

A vote of confidence.

A watched phone never rings.

A watched pot never boils.

Awesome.

A wolf in sheep's clothing.

A woman can do anything a man can.

*A woman's ass and a whiskey glass has made many men
a horse's ass.*

A woman's place is in the home.

"B"

Back at ya.

Back in the day.

Back stabbers.

Back to the old drawing board.

Bad boys, bad boys, what you are gonna do.

Bad company corrupts good character.

Bad news always travels fast.

Bad to the bone.

Bare watching.

Beans, beans good for your heart, the more you eat, the more you fart.

Beating around the bush.

Beauty is in the eye of the beholder.

Beauty's only skin deep.

Be careful about what you wish for, it might come true.

Been there, done that, got the t-shirt and the mug.

Beggars can't be choosers.

Behave yourself.

Behind every strong man, there's a strong woman.

Behold, the only thing greater than yourself. (The Universe)

Being over righteousness or overwise will destroy you.

Believe half of what you see and none of what you hear.

Believe in yourself.

Bend over backward.

Be patient, don't put the cart before the horse.

Be prepared.

Best case scenario.

Be thankful for what you got.

Better death than dishonor.
Bet your booties, granny.
Beware of Greeks bearing gifts.
Beware of what you wish for.
Be yourself, everyone else is already taken.
Be yourself, you can't be anyone else.
Bigger is better.
Bip bam, thank you, ma'am.
Birds do it and fly, cats do it and cry.
Birds of a feather flock together.
Bitch made.
Bite the dust.
Blacker than a coal miners' ass.
Black on black crimes.
Bleeding stuck struck pig.
Blind leading the blind.
Blood counts the most.
Blood is thicker than water.
Booty call.
Boo-Yah.
Born free.
Boss is better than it's told. (Mother)
Boy 'o' boy.
Boys will be boys.
Boy toys.
Braking bread.
Breath kicking like Jackie Chan.
Bring home the bacon.
Broke as a fat kid's big wheel.
Brothers from another mother.

Brown bagger.

Brownie points.

Buckle up.

Bulldagger.

Bullets don't have eyes.

Burning bread on me.

Burning daylight.

Burning the candle at both ends.

Busier than a one-armed paper hanger.

Butterbean, butterboom.

Buyers beware.

Buyers remorse.

Buzzard luck.

By jove, I think he's got it.

By the numbers.

"C"

Call a spade a spade.
Calling a skillet black.
Calm as a cucumber.
Calm before the storm.
Camel's toe. (Vagina)
Candyman, Candyman,... man.
Can hear a rat piss on cotton.
Can I help you?
Can I hit that?
Can we just get along?
Can you dig it?
Can you feel me?
Can you hear me now?
Can you hear the things that are coming out of my mouth?
Can't keep a good man down.
Can't see the forest for the trees.
Can't spare a square. (Toilet paper)
Can't stop progress.
Can't turn a whore into a housewife.
Can't walk a mile in my shoes.
Careful as a fat man crossing a footbridge.
Cash is king.
Casket sharp. (Dressed)
Cat burglars.
Cattle don't graze after sheep.
Caught with your pants down.
Cha-Ching!
Charity starts at home.

Cheaters never win and winners never cheat.

Check your pride at the door.

Chicken coop. (Weight station)

Chicken head.

Chivalry isn't dead.

Choke the chicken. (Urinate)

Choose a job you love, and you will never work a day in your life.

Choose life or choose death.

Clacking hens.

Clean as a pin.

Clean as a whistle.

Clean as emergence.

Close as thieves.

Close as one is to two.

Close but no prize.

Clothes don't make the man, man makes the clothes.

Cocked ace duce.

Cock strong.

Colder than a gold digger's ass in January.

Colder than a well-diggers ass.

Cold war.

Color, equal flavor.

Come and get it.

Come down off the ladder.

Come down off your high horse.

Come hell are high water.

Come to mama.

Come to papa.

Compromise, to a certain extent, become surrender.

Competition is the life of trade.
Condition is everything.
Congradulations!
Control your time and you will control your life.
Cooking with gas.
Cool as a cucumber.
Cooler heads prevail.
Correction does much, but encouragement does more.
Count no man truly happy until he dies.
Cowards die many deaths but the brave only once.
Crack addicts.
Craps. (Dice)
Crash and burn.
Crawl, Walk, Run.
Crazy as a road lizard.
Crazy like a fox.
Crime doesn't pay!
Cross the bridge when you get there, not before.
Cross the tees and dot the eyes.
Crying cleanses the soul.
Curiosity killed the cat.
Cuter than a bug's ear.
Cut the head off a snake, and the body dies.
Cut to the chase.

"D"

Damn, damn, damn.

Damned if you do and damned if you don't.

Danger is real, but fear is a choice.

Deader than a doornail.

Dead man can't talk.

Dead man walking.

Dead money.

Death before dishonor.

Death is inevitable.

Death is permanent.

Death lives in the crack house. (Dope house)

Death smiles at us all, all we can do is smile back.

Delay, is the deadly form of denial.

Desperate situations call for desperate actions.

Destiny is not a matter of chance but of choice.

Diamonds are a girl's best friend.

Diamonds in the rough.

Different strokes for different folks.

Dyn-o-mite.

Discipline is the bridge between goals and accomplishment.

Divisiveness is a sure path to failure.

Does that make sense?

Dog eat dog.

Dogs are man's best friend.

Do it with love.

Dominoe.

Do not shit where you eat.

Do not take life too seriously, you'll never get out alive.

Don't be a sore loser.
Don't believe that fat meat's greasy.
Don't be scared.
Don't bet your life on it.
Don't bite the hand that feeds you.
Don't borrow against the stone.
Don't bring a knife to a gunfight.
Don't burn your bridges.
Don't call me brother.
Don't change horses in the middle of the stream.
Don't count me out.
Don't count your chickens before they hatch.
Don't crowd your luck.
Don't cry because it's over, smile because it happened.
Don't cry over spilled milk.
Don't do as I do, do as I say do.
Don't do nothing I wouldn't do.
Don't drop the ball.
Don't drop the soap.
Don't eat the daisies.
Don't eat yellow snow.
*Don't except any wooden nickels, you might get a splinter
    in your hand.*
Don't fight the war if you can't win.
Don't forget where you came from.
Don't get it twisted.
Don't get mad, get even.
Don't go there!
Don't hate, appreciate.
Don't hate the player, hate the game.

Don't judge a book by its cover.

Don't just follow the path, make your own.

Don't kick a man while he's down.

Don't kid a kidder.

Don't kill the messenger.

Don't know the value of a dollar.

Don't let nothing stick to your hands. (Mother)

Don't let the bed bug's bite.

Don't let the Jones get you down.

Don't let the streetlights catch you not at home. (Mother)

Don't let your Monday ruin your Sunday.

Don't let your mouth overload your ass.

Don't let yourself indulge in vain wishes.

Don't let your tomorrow ruin your today.

Don't look a gift horse in the mouth.

Don't look back, something may be gaining on you.

Don't panic.

Don't poke the bear.

Don't quit your day job.

Don't rain on my parade.

Don't rock the boat.

Don't shoot the messenger.

Don't speak until you're spoken to.

Don't stare a gift horse in the mouth.

Don't start anything and it won't be anything.

Don't start none, won't be none.

Don't start nothing you can't finish.

Don't take a knife to a gunfight.

Don't take it personally.

Don't trust NOBODY.

Don't use a cannon to kill a mosquito.

Don't walk under ladders.

Dopefiends.

Do the unexpected.

Double jeopardy.

Do what you know and know what you do.

Do what you say, say what you mean.

Down by law.

Dreams are like repressed desires of the things we wish for.

Dress to impress.

Drop a dime.

Dropped like a bad habit.

Duce is wild.

Ducking One Time. (The Police)

Dumb and Dumber.

Dumb as a box of rocks.

"E"

Early bird catches the worm.

Early word gets the bird.

Earn your keep.

Easy as slapping on a new coat of paint.

Easy as water off a duck back.

Easy come easy go.

Easy greasy, you got a long way to slide.

Education is not preparation for life, education is life itself.

Eggs running like Micheal Johnson.

Ego drives the train.

Emotions can sometimes overrule logic.

Enjoying the fruits of my labors.

Enough is as good as a feast.

Escape goat.

Even a blind squirrel can find a nut once in a while.

Even a coyote will fight back if he's cornered.

Even if you're on the right track, you'll get run over if you just sit there.

Everybody has a story.

Everybody has the right to be a sucker once.

Everybody is a star.

Every cloud has a silver lining.

Every day brings new choices.

Every dog has its day and a good dog has two.

Every man dies, not every man lives.

Every one can change.

Every one has a price, you just have to find out what it is.

Every one who got where he is had to begin where he was.

Every rose has its thorns.

Everything has a beginning, a middle and an end.

Everything has a price.

Everything in life is luck.

Everything in life has been figured out, but how to live.

Everything that glitters ain't gold.

Everything that's mine is yours.

Every snake has two fangs.

Excuses are like assholes, everybody has one.

Expecting the worst hoping for the best.

Expect the unexpected.

Experience is not what happens to you, it's what you do with what happens to you.

Experience is the best teacher.

Executive Clemency.

Eyes are the mirrors to the soul.

Eyes are the windows into the soul.

"F"

Fab four. (The Beatles)

Fagget.

Faint heart never won fair maiden. (Cervantes)

Fall down seven times, stand up eight.

Fare exchange ain't no robbery.

Father knows best.

Fear is nothing but a feeling, it can kill you like hot and cold.

Feed a cold.

Feed um with a long-handled spoon. (Mother)

Feelings change, memories don't.

Feel the need for speed.

Fighting the good fight.

Finders keepers, losers weepers.

Fine as C&H grain sugar.

Fine as frog's hair.

Fine wine mellows with age.

Finger licking good.

Fire it up.

First impressions are important.

First in peace, first in war.

Fish is brain food.

Flip the script.

Flying blind.

Focus on the prize.

Food for thought.

Fools rush in where wise men fear to tread.

For argument sake.

Forget the things which have passed.
Forget me not.
For lack of a better term.
For whom the bells tow? They tow for thee.
For every action, there's a reaction.
Forged by fire.
For those who don't remember the past are
    condemned to repeat it.
Forty acres and a mule.
Freedom is the result of sacrifice.
Free falling. (Wearing no underwear)
Friday the thirteenth.
Friends are a blessing.
Friendship isn't what you say, it's what you do.
From the errors of others, a wise man corrects his own.
From the first slap and cry, we all start to die.
From the rooter to the tooter.
From the womb to the tomb.
Fruits of your labors.
Fuck you!

"G"

Gambling is for losers.

Game changer.

Game recognize game.

Gave me the bird.

Gay.

Georgia peach.

Get all your ducks in a row.

Get busy living are getting busy dying.

Get down on it.

Get in where you fit in.

Get off your high horse.

Get over it.

Get strapped. (Gun)

Get up, get out and get something.

Ghetto fabulous.

Gift of gab.

Girl, you got more curves than a bottle of coke.

Git 'er did.

Git in - where - you fit in.

Git up, git out, and get something.

Give back.

Give me a break.

Give me five.

Give me Liberty or give me Death.

Give the devil some.

Give the drummer some.

Give them a foot, and they'll take a mile.

Give them an inch, and they'll take a mile.

Give them enough rope, and they'll hang themselves.

Give umm a break.

Give umm hell.

Go big are go home.

Go down swinging.

Go figure.

Going Dutch.

Going for bad.

Going to party like it's 1999.

Going to pick a bone with you.

Gone but not forgotten.

Gone fishing.

Good fences make good neighbors.

Good for nothing.

Good guys finish last.

Good luck.

Good news cancels out bad news.

Good night Irene.

Good things come to those who wait.

Good things never die.

Good to go.

Goody two shoes.

Goose is a goose, nenny nenny if it wasn't for kinfolks, I wouldn't have gotten any.

Got buzzard luck.

Got my fingers crossed.

Got jokes?

Go to Hell.

Gotta pess like a boar hog.

Got to go and pinch a load. (Bowel movement)

Got up on the wrong side of the bed.

Go screw yourself.

Grab the bull by the horns and get her done.

Greased palms.

Great minds think alike.

Greed will imprison us all.

Greenbacks. (Dollar bills)

Growing mole like a peach dish.

Guns don't kill people, bullets and people kill people.

Gut-wrenching.

"H"

Hand is quicker than the eye.

Handle your business.

Hang on in there.

Happier than a bumble bee in a flower patch.

Happiness is a choice.

Happy Anniversary!

Happy Birthday!

Happy days are here again.

Hard as times in '29.

Hard headed as a pine board knot.

Haters gonna hate.

Hava look-see.

Have a look-see.

Have you lost your marbles?

Have your ducks in a row.

Head is hard as a pinewood box.

Head strong.

Health is everything.

Heap see and few know.

He is and she is a crossdresser.

Heartache and heartbreak are a part of life.

Hears mud in your eyes.

Hear today and gone tomorrow.

He bears watching.

Heep sees, and few know.

Hell hath no fury as a woman scorned.

Hell no!

He'll talk you to Death.

He's as crooked as the letter "S."

He's a good haggler.

He's a gunslinger. (Large penis)

He's a mac daddy.

He's got vertigo.

He's my right-hand man.

He's on a guilt trip.

He's so scared, he outran a telephone call.

He who controls Gold rules. So the Golden Rule.

He who hesitates will lose.

He who knows and knows that he knows is a wise man, listen for there you WILL learn something.

He who laughs last laughs the loudest.

He who lies, the mouth gets dry.

Hey dude, you're screwed.

Higher than a Georgia pine in June.

Highway robbery.

Hit and run just for fun.

Hit it and quit it.

Hit it out of the park.

Hit the ground running.

Hit the hay.

Hobby lobby.

Hog tied.

Holly macaroni.

Home slice.

Home sweet home.

Homo.

Honesty is the best policy.

Honky.

Honor among thieves.

Honest Indian.

Hooker. (Prostitute)

Hope for the best, expect the worst.

Hope is a good thing, and a good thing never dies.

Hotter than fish grease.

How can we lose with the stuff we use?

How do you like me now?

How sweet it is.

Hump day.

Hurry up and wait.

Hustling.

"I"

I ain't got eye water to cry with.

I already know.

I bend over backwards for you.

I can read you like a book.

Icing on the cake.

I'd die without you.

I'd rather be caught with it than without it. (A Gun)

I double dog dare you.

I doubt that.

If a man doesn't have anything he'd die for, he doesn't deserve to live.

If anything is worth having, it's worth fighting for.

If at first you don't succeed, try and try again.

I feel so bad, feel like a ball game on a rainy day.

If I coulda, shoulda, woulda.

If I'm lying, I'm flying.

If I only had a nickel for every time, I heard that.

If it doesn't fit, don't force it.

If it doesn't fit, you must acquit.

If it looks like a duck, walks like a duck, and sounds like a duck, it must be a duck.

If I tell you a chicken dips snuff, look under the wing and find the box. (Mother)

If I tell you, I have to kill you.

If it seems too good to be untrue, it usually is.

If it's not one thing, it's another.

If it's not your business, shut up.

If it sounds too good to be true, then it's not.

If if it sounds to good to be true, it is to good to be true.

If it walks like a duck and quacks like a duck, it's a duck.

If it wasn't for bad luck, I would have no luck at all.

If looks could kill.

If shit was brains, yours wouldn't even smell.

If the shoe fits, wear it.

If this world was mine.

If you build it, they will come.

If you can't be good, be careful. (Mother)

If you can't hold a job you need to change your line of work.

If you can't keep quiet, shut up.

If you can't love the one you want, love the one you with.

If you can't hit where you aim, sit down.

If you can't stand the heat, stay out of the kitchen.

If you can't say nothing nice, don't say anything at all.

If you don't know, you don't know.

If you don't learn from your mistakes, you're doomed to repeat them.

If you don't like the weather, just wait ten minutes and it will change.

If you feel froggy, then jump.

If you forget from where you came, you will lose what you got.

If you give an inch, they take a mile.

If you give em enough rope, they'll hang themselves.

If you have to ask, you can't afford it.

If you look for trouble, you'll find it.

If you love something, set it free.

If you mess with the bull, you'll get the horns.

If you play, you will pay.

If you raise your voice and it doesn't do anything, well, it's time to use your hand.

If you're looking for something to be jealous about, you'll find it.

If you stand for nothing, you'll fall for anything.

If you talk all the time, you got to be right.

If you want it to taste good, put your foot in it.

If walls could talk.

Ignorance is bliss.

Ignorant men raise questions that wise men answered a thousand years ago.

I got your six.

I had a lot on my plate.

I'll beat you like you stole something.

I'll drink to that.

I'll holla.

I love it when a good plan comes together.

I'm a bad man.

I made my lady.

I'm a team player.

Imagination is the mother of invention.

I'm at the end of my rope.

I'm ass out.

I'm dead set on that.

I'm going to clean your clock.

I'm going to drop you like a hot potato.

I'm going to drop you like third period french.

I'm in like Flynn.

I'm just saying.

I'm mad as hell, and I'm not going to take it anymore.
I'm only human.
I'm with you from the womb to the tomb.
"I'm sorry," I know that already.
In hell or high water.
In order to be the man, you have to beat the man.
In the black.
In the doghouse.
In the heat of the night.
In the red.
In the thick of things.
In wine, there's truth.
I pinky swear.
I pity the fool.
I read you like a book.
Iron sharpens iron.
Is a glass half full more than a glass half empty?
Is fat meat greasy?
I shall not tell a lie.
Is it like that?
Is pigs pussy pork?
I surround myself with positive, productive people of goodwill and decency.
It ain't what you do, it's who you know.
It can't get any worst.
It doesn't matter what you do in life, just be the best you can.
I think anything is possible if you have the mindset, the will, and desire to do it and put the time in.
I think I just got hit by a bus.

I thought you knew.

It isn't over till the fat lady sings.

It is what it is.

It must be jelly because jam doesn't shake like that.

It never fails.

It's a dog-eat-dog world.

It's a done deal.

It's a honey hole.

It's a Kodak moment.

It's a long row to hoe.

It's always darkest before the dawn.

It's a man's world.

It's a no-brainer.

It's a part of life.

It's apples and oranges.

It's a rainy night in Georgia.

It's a small world.

It's as sound as a dollar.

It's better to be called a fool than to open your mouth and erase all doubt.

It's better to give till it hurts.

It's better to have and not need than to need and not have.

It's better to have loved and lost than to have not loved at all.

It's better to think than to lust.

It's bitter-sweet.

It's cold as a gold digger's ass.

It's come full circle.

It's easy to beg for permission than to ask forgiveness.

It's "finger-licking good."

It's good to have a dream to follow.
It's harder to be a father than to become one.
It's like apples and oranges.
It's like getting gum on your shoe. (Always there)
It's like putting a $2.00 ring in a $50.00 box.
It's lonely at the top, but you eat better.
It smells a little fishy.
It's my way are the highway.
It's nice when a plan comes together.
It's not how you win are lose but how you play the game.
It's not the length of life but the depth of it.
It's not the size of the boat but the motion of the ocean.
It's not the size of the dog in the fight but the size of the fight in the dog.
It's not what you are, it's what people think you are.
It's not what you look at that matters, it's what you see.
It's on like a pot of neck bones.
It's on like donkey kong.
It's on.
It's on me.
It's on you.
It's raining, men.
It's the empty barrels that make the most noise.
It's the fate of glass to break.
It's tighter than a miser.
It's tighter than Dick's hatband.
It's tighter than a frog's pussy, and you know that's waterproof.
It's time to take cookies when cookies are passed.
It's water over the bridge.

It's water under the bridge.

It's what I do.

It's you cheater, who's more afraid of being cheated.

It's your thang, do what you wanna do.

It takes a crook to catch a crook.

It takes a village to raise a child.

It takes one to know one.

It takes two to tangle.

I want to be free!

I wasn't born yesterday.

I wouldn't touch you with a ten-foot pole.

I work hard for the money.

I've fallen and I can't get up.

I've got good news and bad news.

I've got the blues.

I've learned my lesson.

"J"

Jack of all trades, master of none. Never concurs much.

Jailbait.

Jaw jacking.

Joy is when you realize how good GOD is.

Joy ride.

Jumpin' Jupiter.

Jumping the broom. (Marriage)

Junk in the trunk.

Junk is something that cannot make a contribution to you.

Just a dog in a manger.

Just chilling.

Just grasping at straws.

Justice is blind.

Just when I thought I was out, they pulled me back in.
    (God Father)

"K"

Keep between the ditches. (Stay on the road)

Keep it in the family.

Keep it on the down-low.

Keep it real.

Keep it simple.

Keep keeping on.

Keep me in the loop.

Keep on pushing.

Keep on trucking.

Keep reaching for the stars.

Keep the blinds shut.

Keep your karma clean.

Keep your eyes on the brass ring.

Keep your eyes on the prize.

Keep your friends close and your enemies closer.

Keep your head up.

Keep your heart open, and love will always find its way in.

Kicking ass and taking names.

Kickin like a chicken.

Kick the bucket.

*Kids are like bowling balls, you have to let them go and
    hope they don't go in the gutter.*

Kill, or be killed.

Kill two birds with one stone.

Kiss my ass.

Knight in shining armor.

Knocking her boots. (Having sex)

Knock on somebody. (Snitch)

Knock on wood.
Knowledge is power.
Known by many, loved by all.
Kraut. (German)

"L"

Last long as a candle in the wind.

Law of average says.

Laying down on the job.

Learn to listen because opportunity sometimes knock softly.

Leave them wanting more.

Left holding the bag.

Let bygones be bygones.

Let it ride.

Let me put a bug in your ear.

Let the buyer beware. (Caveat Emptor)

Let the doorknob hit you where the good LORD split you.

Let the party begin.

Let the door hit you where the LORD split you.

Let um land where they fall.

Lets agree to disagree.

Lets cut to the chase.

Lets get married.

Lets Go Dutch.

Let sleeping dogs lie.

Let the chips fall where they may.

Let your imagination run wild.

Liar, Liar pants on fire.

Life consists not only of good cards but of playing the ones you have well.

Life is a bowl of cherries.

Life is a game of inches.

Life is a great sweet song, start the music. (Ronald Reagan)

Life is like a baseball game, three strikes you're out.

Life is like a box of chocolates, you never know what you gonna get.

Life is like a wheelbarrow, you get nowhere till you start pushing. So, Press on.

Life is what you make it to be.

Life loves the liver of it.

Life of the party.

Life rewards the courageous few.

Life's about change.

Life well spent is long.

Lightning doesn't strike twice in the same spot.

Like a duck on a june bug.

Like a kid in a candy shop.

Like a moth to a flame.

Like a piece, of gum stuck to the bottom of your shoe, it's always there.

Like a rooster threw the corn.

Like dropping a stone in a creek, you don't know where the ripples are going to stop.

Like father, like son.

Like riding a bike, you never forget.

Like shooting duck's in a barrel.

Like shooting fish in a barrell.

Like tough shoe leather, hard to wear out.

Like trying to find hair on a frog.

Like two peas in a pod.

Like water off a ducks back.

Live and let live.

Live life to the fullest, and focus on the positive.

Live to fight another day.

Live with it.

Living a secret is like living a lie, it destroys and kills.

Living from paycheck to paycheck.

Living high on the hog.

Living large.

Loaded for bear.

Lock, stock and barrel.

LOL. (Laugh out loud, lots of luck)

Look before you leap.

Look, but don't touch.

Looking like a cookie cutter.

Looking for closure.

Looking ramrod straight.

Loose lips sink ships.

Loser.

Lots of love.

Love at first sight.

Love, at first sight, is often cured by a second look.

Love conquers all.

Love is a hurting thing.

Love is impulsive.

Love is like measles, you only get it once.

Love is like war, easy to begin but very hard to stop.

Love is mutual weirdness.

Love isn't something you find, love is something that finds you.

Love isn't what you say but what you do.

Love makes the world go round.

Love, peace, and soul.

Love, peace, justice, and equality.

"M"

Make a long story short.

Make it rain.

Make love, not war.

Make my ass want a dip of stuff.

Make you want to smack your mama.

Make no bones about it.

Make peace from the past and try to live with it.

Makes me no never mind.

Make sense?

Make someone happy and you'll be happy too.

Make sure the shoe fits.

Make you an offer you can't refuse. (Godfather)

Make your bed hard, you will sleep in it. (Mother)

Make you wanna smack your mama.

Making a baby doesn't make you a man or a woman.

Making a mountain out of a molehill.

Making mistakes is the way to learn.

Making money just makes cents.

Making money under the table.

Making people laugh is like giving them a vacation.

Mama said there would be days like this.

Man cave.

Man is only great when he acts from passion.

Mano a mano. (Correct)

Mans got to know his limitations.

Man that grabs little fish scares big fish away.

Man, the top of the food chain.

Man to man.

Man up.

Many hands make light work.

Mean what you say, say what you mean.

Measure twice, cut once.

Mediocre is settling between failure and success.

Memories don't change.

Mentally challenged.

Mess with the bull, and you might get the horns.

Method in the madness.

Mind your own business.

Mirrors don't lie, fortunately, they don't laugh.

Misery loves company.

Mama said there'll be days like this.

Money begets money.

Money can't buy you, love.

Money doesn't change you, it changes the people around you.

Money is no problem.

Money is the root of all EVIL.

Money's in the details.

Money talks and bull-shit walks.

More money, more problems.

More than a mouth full is a waste.

Moss always grows on the north side of the tree. (In the northern hemisphere)

Most definitely.

Mother's love, Mothers love.

Mowing the lawn. (A search patterns.)

Muddy the water.

Murphy's Law. (Will happen)

Music soothes from the savage beast.
My bad.
My boo.
My brother.
My business is nobody's business.
My Johnson. (Penis)
My mind was playing tricks on me.
My M.O.
My niggar.
My optimism wears heavy boots and is loud.
My pleasure.
My silent partner.
My whip. (Car)
My word is bond.

"N"

Nail your hide to the barnyard door.

Nap trap. (Rest stop)

Narrow-minded.

Natural born killer.

Nature wins.

Necessity is the mother of invention.

Negative people make positive people positively sick.

Nigga.

Nigger.

Nervous as a fish out of water.

Nervous as a long tail cat in a room full of rocking chairs.

Nervuos as a whore in church.

Never a second chance to make a first impression.

Never be the last to leave the party.

Never bite off more than you can chew.

Never cease to amaze me.

Never count your chickens before they hatch.

Never fear going forward slowly, fear standing still.

Never eat yellow snow.

Never forget where you come from.

Never give a sucker an even break.

Never give up, give out of trying.

Never give up on a good thing.

Never go looking for trouble.

Never make a nuisance of yourself by asking favors, people always want to be paid back.

Never mistake bravery with good sense.

Never miss a meal, Bill and Jill.

Never lend more than you can stand to give. (Father)

Never let anyone do more for you than can you do for them. (Myself)

Never let anyone steal your joy.

Never let a woman beat your hand out.

Never let the right hand know what the left hand is doing. (Mother)

Never let um see you sweat.

Never neglect any possibilities.

Never put all your eggs in one basket.

Never put off today for tomorrow because tomorrow isn't promised. (Mother)

Never say die.

Never say never.

Never send a boy to do a man's job.

Never sign without reading.

Never spit in the wind.

Never talk business are women with a stranger.

Never talk with your mouth full.

Never tear down your bridges, you might have to cross them again. (Mother)

Never too old to learn.

Never trust a big butt and a smile.

Never trust anyone, not even me. (Father)

Never trust a plumber with cloth gloves.

Never worry about what you're going to get, just show them what you can do.

Nice guys finish last.

Nigger, please!

No contract, no money back.

No credit.

No crime goes unpunished.

No cure, no pay.

No doubt.

No good deed goes unpunished.

No guts, no glory.

No harm, no foul.

No hatred is rage like a woman scorned.

No honor amongst thieves.

No justice, no peace.

No man is an island.

No, means no!

No monkey business.

No news is good news.

Nonviolence.

No one can make you feel inferior without your consent.

No one is above the law.

No one loves a loser.

No one is born with intolerance, it has to be taught.

No one will help you if you don't help yourself.

No pain, no gain.

No rest for the weary.

No risk, no reward.

No shoes, no shirt, NO SERVICE.

Not by age but by knowledge is wisdom acquired.

No time like the present.

Not for the faint of heart.

Nothing beats a failure but a try.

Nothing better than a friend.

Nothing but space and opportunity.

Nothing comes to a sleeper but a dream, and when he awakes, it's gone. (Myself)

Nothing from nothing leaves nothing.

Nothing lasts forever.

Nothing that you have not given away will never be really yours.

Nothings impossible.

Nothings unfair that happens.

Nothing ventured, nothing gained.

Not responding.

Not so fast!

No way, hosea.

No way to go but up.

No way, Jose.

Now you're talking.

No, you did-ent.

Numero uno.

"O"

Often imitated but never duplicated.

Oh, no!

One of the most important things in life is showing up.

Ole what a deadly web we weave when we practice deceiving.

Ole what a tangled web we weave when we practice deceiving.

Older the violin the sweeter the music.

Old fools used to be young fools.

Old, is when you get compliments for your alligator shoes and you're barefooted.

Old so-in-so.

On a clear day, you can see forever.

On a need-to-know basis.

Once a cheat, always a cheat.

Once a man, twice a child.

Once a Marine, always a Marine.

Once a month, bleeding bitch.

Once a thief, always a thief.

Once mine always mine.

Once the arrow leaves the bow, it's too late to change the aim.

Once you don't succeed, try, try again.

Once you get mad, you lose.

Once you go black, you never go back.

Once you pour water from a bottle, it's not easy to get it back in.

Once the dust settles.

One bad apple can spoil the whole barrel.

One bad apple spoils the whole bunch.

One bad thing about doing nothing, you can't take a day off.

One born every minute.

One compliment deserves another.

One day at a time.

One for the money, two for the show, three to get ready to go, man, go.

One hand washes the other.

On GOD's green earth.

On hard times.

One foot in the grave.

One man's loss is another man's gain.

One man's trash is another man's treasure.

One must count on oneself.

One nation under God.

One of a kind.

One on one.

One timer. (Police)

Only in America.

Only the rich and strong survive.

On point.

On the real.

On the top of your game.

On your mark, get ready, go.

Oops there it is.

Open a can of whip-ass on you.

Open and shut case.

Opening a whole new can of worms.

Opportunity is the mother of reinvention.

Opportunity is the room in which you step.

Organization is key.

Ours is not to reason why, ours is, but to do are die.

Out of sight, out of mind.

Out of the mouths of babes.

Out of the skillet into the fire.

Over burdened.

Over confidence and pride can kill a person faster than a bullet.

"P"

Pain always leaves a gift.

Papa was a rolling stone.

Parting is such sweet sorrow. (Romeo and Juliet)

Partly cloudy are partly sunny.

Patience is a virtue.

Pay attention!

Pay backs a bitch.

Pay you no, never mind.

Peckerwood. (White man)

People in hell want ice water.

People living in glass houses shouldn't throw no stones.

People make the world go round.

People would rather see you sad than happy. So, keep smiling. (Mother)

People under the influence stand out.

People who don't fail are people who don't try.

People will never forget how you made them feel.

Perfection is boring.

Perseverance is the best exercise of character.

Pick on someone your own size.

Pictures never lie.

Pimp are die.

Pimping ain't easy.

Pinch me, I must be dreaming.

Pinky swears.

Playing both sides against the middle.

Play on the square.

Play for keeps.

Played for the love of the game.

Play to win.

Please don't eat the daisies.

Poetry in motion.

Poker face.

Politics are the art of the impossible.

Politics makes strange bedfellows.

Poor white trash.

Positive anything is better than negative nothing.

Positive thinking will let you do everything better than negative thinking will.

Poverty comes through the door and love goes out the window.

Power corrupts.

Practice makes perfect unless you're practicing wrong.

Prepare for war in a time of peace. (Mother)

Pride goes before fall.

Proofs in the pudding.

Proof of the pudding is in the eating.

Prouder than a game rooster.

Pulling up stakes.

Pull your own weight.

Pull your pants up and be a MAN.

Pussy whipped.

Put it in your pipe and smoke it. (Mother)

Put that on something.

Putting the cart before the horse.

Put your best foot forward.

Put your foot in your mouth.

"Q"

Queen Bee.

Quicker than a sailor on shore leave.

Quit complaining and do something about it.

Quit while you're ahead.

Quite as a field mouse.

Quite before the storm.

Quite, I'm trying to sleep.

Quite, please.

Quitters never win, and winners never lose.

"R"

Ran out on a rail.

Reach for the stars.

Realm of possibilities.

Redneck. (Good ole country boys)

Redskins. (Indians)

Regrets and death mean you have done something wrong.

Regret the things you've done than the things you haven't done.

Remember the Alamo.

Remember the Titans.

Rest and relaxation.

Right.

Right as fireworks on the fourth of July.

Right as rain.

Right from the start.

Right hand, man.

Right on.

Right on the tip of my tongue.

Right place, wrong time.

Ring tailed-leader.

Riots are the language of the unheard. (M.L.K.)

Road dog.

Road kill.

Rob Peter to pay Paul. (Mother)

Rob the cradle.

Rolling in clover.

Rome wasn't built in a day.

Roses are red, violets are blue...
Run of the mill.
Running around like a chicken with its head cut off.
Rust never sleeps.

"S"

Safety first.

Salers remorse.

Same thing that makes you laugh will makes you cry.

Save a penny and a dollar will grow.

Saved by the bell.

Save face.

Saving dollars just make cents.

Say what you mean and mean what you say.

Scarce as frog's hair.

Scarce as hen's teeth.

Scared as a whore in church.

Scared shitless.

Scared straight.

Schmuck.

Seeing is believing.

See you later, alligator after a while crocodile.

Separate the men from the boys.

Serious as a heart attack.

Serve and protect.

Set it off.

Sex sells!

Shades of gray.

Shake hands with the president. (Urinate)

Shallow-minded people.

Sharper than an Arkansas sprinter.

She draws men like fish to bate.

*She was like a swiss clock, the same movement over and
    over.*

She's all that and a pot of grits.
She's a snowflake. (White girl)
She's a tall drink of water.
She shuck.
She shed.
She's open as a hunting season.
She's open like 7-11.
She works hard for the money.
Shinnier than a diamond in a goat's ass.
Ships that pass in the night.
Shit fire and save the matches.
Shit for brains.
Shit happens.
Shock and awe.
Show me some love.
Shop till you drop.
Sho, you right! (Myself)
Should I, Would I, Could I.
Show me. (Mo.'s motto)
Shut the front door. (Shut the fuck up)
Shut your mouth when you hear grown folks talking.
Signed, sealed, delivered.
Silence is golden.
Silent partner.
Silly rabbit tricks are for kids.
Simply a means to an end.
Since Skip was a punk.
Sink or swim.
Size does matter.
Size doesn't matter.

Skaggs. (Broke bitches)

Skainks. (Ugly bitches)

Skeletons in your closet.

Sky's the limit.

Slant eyes. (Chinese)

Slower than a banker agreeing to a cash loan.

Small as a mosquito peter. (Myself)

Smile and the world smile with you.

Smiles are free.

Smooth as silk.

Smoother than a baby's butt.

Snake eyes.

Sneak thieves.

Snitches get stitches.

Snowflake. (White girl)

Snoozers are losers.

S.O.B.

Social distancing.

Soft as a baby's bottom.

Soft as medicated cotton.

Some folks are wise, and some are otherwise.

Some like it hot.

Some people are beyond saving.

Some people say if you get caught on film you'll lose your soul.

Something old, something new, something borrowed and something blue.

Something worth blowing your horns about.

Sometimes cheap is a little more expensive.

Sometimes laughter is the best medicine.

Sometimes less is more.

Sometimes peace is through strength.

Sometimes the heart sees what is invisible to the eye.

Sometimes there's a good reason for a man to change his mind.

Sometimes, truth is stranger than fiction.

Sometimes you bend with the breeze, or you break.

Sometimes you have to give up your Queen to win the game.

Sometimes you have to let a man find his way.

Sometimes you win, and sometimes you lose.

Sometimes your past won't let you go.

Son-of-a-bitch.

Son-of-a-biscuit eater. (Mr. Emmett)

Sorry don't get it done.

Sorry is a sorry word.

SOUL is a feeling, not a color.

Sound as a dollar.

Sounds like a plan.

Sowing your wild oats.

Space race.

Speak to the problem, not about the problem.

Spick. (Hispanic)

Squeal like a stuck pig.

Stand by your man.

Starving like Marvin.

Steady as she goes.

Steer it and clear it. (In an accident)

Step on a crack, break your mama's back.

Stick a fork in him, he's done.

Sticks and stones may break my bones but words can never hurt me.

Still water runs deep.

Straight as a mosquitoes peter during mating season.

Straighten up and fly right.

Straight from the horse's mouth.

Stranger danger.

Stolen kisses are always the sweetest.

Strike while the fire is hot. (Mother)

Stone-cold killers.

Stop acting your shoe size.

Stop and smell the roses.

Stop shooting your mouth off.

Study long, study wrong. (Making a decision)

Students ready, the teacher appears.

Sucking hind tit.

Success can be bitter-sweet.

Success is failure turned inside out.

Survey says! (Richard Dawson)

Survival makes people do some things that they know are wrong.

Survival of the fittest.

Sweating like a one-legged man in an ass kicking contest.

Sweating like a whore in church.

Sweating me like a ten-dollar wig.

Swollen down by her colon.

Symplicity is its own artistry.

"T"

Take it easy greasy, you got a long way to slide.
Take it with a grain of salt.
Take life easy, and you'll live a lot longer.
Take the bitter with the sweet.
Take the good with the bad.
Take the money and run.
Take your thumb off the scales.
Talking out the side of your mouth.
Talking shit.
Talk is cheap, you have to do something.
Tared and feathered.
Teamwork makes a dream work. (Lavon James)
Tender as a mother love.
That fish is four days old, and I'm not buying it.
That money's burning a hole in your pocket. (Mother)
That smell will gag a maggot on a gut wagon.
That's a done deal.
That's all I'm saying.
That's all she wrote.
That's awesome.
That't crazy.
That's how the cookie crumbles.
That's on you.
That's music to my ears.
That's my dog.
That's my excuse, and I'm sticking to it.
That's my story, and I'm sticking to it.
That's what I do.

That's what I said.

That's what they say.

That's what's up.

That's water under the bridge.

The acorn doesn't fall far from the tree.

The American dream.

The apple doesn't fall far from the tree.

The ball is in your court.

The best time to buy is when there's blood on the streets.

The best things in life are free.

The best way to learn is to make a mistake.

The bigger they come, the harder they fall.

The birds and the bees.

The bitterest truth is better than the sweetest lie.

The blind leading the blind.

The blacker the berry the sweeter the juice.

The boogieman.

The boneyard.

The boys of summer.

The breadwinner.

The buck stops here.

The cats in the bag and the bags in the river.

The courage of life is a mixture of triumph and tragedy.

The cruelest lies are often told in silence.

The customer is always right.

The dangerous thing in the world is the man who has nothing to lose.

The decisions you make today can have serious consequences.

The Devil made me do it.

The Devil wears parda.
The dogs of war.
The early bird catches the worm.
The empty the pot, the faster it boils.
The ends justify the means.
The face that launched a thousand ships.
The fact of the matter is.
The first time on me, the next time on you.
The fruits of your labor.
The fox ain't worth the chase.
The game doesn't stop. The players change.
The gift of gab.
The glass is half empty.
The glass is half full.
The good and the bad times.
The good die young.
The good, the bad and the ugly.
The grass is always greener on the other side.
The grass is not always greener on the other side.
The haves and the have nots.
The heart of a lion.
The heart was made to be broken.
The heat is on.
The highs and lows.
The house always wins.
The Jack of all trades.
The life you save, maybe your own.
The luck of the draw.
The luck of the Irish.
The man.

Them Bushwhackers.

The method and the madness.

The missing link.

The money's in the detail.

The more you learn, the more you don't know.

The more you see, the more you want.

The more things change, the more they stay the same.

The most important things in life are free.

Them who trades liberties for securities, doesn't deserve either one.

The nature of the beast.

The next time you're at Walmart, buy you some business.

The odds are.

The only disability in life is a bad attitude.

The only good Indian is a dead Indian.

The older she is, the easier she is to catch.

The older the violin, the sweeter the music.

The ole Union Jack.

The only difference between men and boys is the price of their toys.

The only disability in life is a bad attitude.

The only good Indian is a dead Indian.

The only good thing for the trial of the evil is that good men do nothing.

The only three things for sure are taxes, death, and trouble.

The orgasm is a woman's joy and a man's seal of approval.

The patience of a Mexican Saint.

The Peter Pan syndrome, won't grow up.

The pen is mightier than the sword.

The pigeon drops.

The plan is foolproof.

The pot calling the kettle black.

The pudding is never as good as thinking about it.

The punch lines.

The purpose of life is a life of purpose.

The purpose of life is to be happy.

The pursuit of happiness.

The rains in Spain, falls mainly on the plains.

The rich get richer, the poor get poorer.

The ring-tailed leader.

The rollers. (Police)

The roof, the roof, the roof is on fire, we don't need no water let the F.M. burn.

The salt of the earth.

The school of hard knocks.

The seventh son of the seventh son.

The short end of the stick.

The show me state.

The show must go on.

The sky's the limit.

The smoking guns.

The talk of the town.

The tip of the iceberg.

There is just one life for each of us, our own.

There it is.

There's a difference in what people say than what they mean.

There's a fly in the ointment.

There's always one beautiful child in every family and every mother has it.

There's light at the end of the tunnel.

There's a limit to everything but foolishness.

There's always room at the top.

There's a new sheriff in town.

There's a pot of gold at the end of the rainbow.

There's a sucker born every minute.

There's a thousand ways to slice a grape.

There's more fish in the sea.

There's more than one fish in the sea.

There's more than one way to skin a cat.

There's no fool like an old fool.

There's no limit to what a man will do for money, but there is no limit to what he will do for Love.

There's no loss without some gain.

There's no place like home.

There's no such thing as a free ride.

There's no time like the present.

There's nothing for sure in life but taxes, death, and trouble.

There's nothing more dangerous than an honest man.

There's nothing predictable when a husband is betrayed.

There's one born every minute.

There's strength in numbers.

The skillet calling the kettle black.

The third time the charm.

Three's a crowd.

The train has left the station.

The way to a man's heart is through his stomach.

The way to Love anything is to realize it may be lost.

The whole nine yards.

The whole world is a stage, and everybody plays a part.

The whole world is a stage. It's the acting that matters.

The world keeps turning.

The worst-case scenario.

The writings on the wall.

They didn't just walk off. (Stolen things)

They're Boston strong.

They're not on the same page.

They're on the same page.

They said it couldn't be done.

They say.

They walk the walk and talk the talk.

Thick as flies.

Thick as thieves.

Things that are not what they appear to be, are otherwise.

Things happen for a reason.

This is going to hurt you more than it will me.

This is how we roll.

This isn't my first rodeo.

This is some bullshit.

Three hots and a cot.

Throwing dirt.

Throwing good money after bad.

Throwing smoking mirrors.

Thru pain, there's peace.

Tickled pink.

Tickled to death.

Tidy whities

Tight as frog pussy and you know that's waterproof.

Till the cows comes home.

Time brings about a change.

Time flies when you're having fun.

Time heals all wounds.

T.L.C.

To be the champion, you have to beat the champion.

To be, are not to be, that is the question.

To be free is to have achieved your life.

Today is the first day of the rest of your life.

To bet on things, you have to have a closed mind.

To each his own.

To faced.

Together we stand, divided we fall. (Saxon)

To legit to quit.

To little, too late.

To many cooks spoils the soup.

Tomorrow never comes.

Top dog.

Top of the line.

Top of the morning.

Top shelf.

Tore up from the floor up. (Intoxicated)

To succeed in life, you need two things. ignorance and confidence.

To the moon Alice.

To the victor goes the spoils.

Tougher than a piece of wet leather.

Tougher than two yellow toenails.

Tough times don't last, tough people do.

Touch base with me.

Towelhead. (Iranian)

Trailor trash.

Trouble is easy to get in but hard to get out of.

True dat.

Truth can be stranger than fiction.

Truth is the measure of a man.

Trust me.

Try it, you'll like it.

Try to be a rainbow in someone's cloud.

Trying to make a dollar out of fifteen cents.

Trying to make a mountain out of a molehill.

Turning white with fear.

Turn out the lights, the party's over.

Turn over a new leaf.

Turtleneck. (Penis)

Two's a company, and there's a crowd.

"U"

Up shit creek without a paddle.

Up the creek without a paddle.

Umm is not an answer.

Uncommon valor.

Understanding is the best thing in the world.

Unfaithful.

United we stand, divided we fall. (Patrick Henry)

Use it are losing it. (Vacation time)

"V"

Variety is the spice of life that gives us flavor.
Victors win, victims lose.
Virtue is its own rewards.

"W"

Wall flower.

Want in one hand, shit in another and see which one gets filled the quickest. (Mother)

W.A.R. is HELL.

War, money, and politics.

W.A.R.! what is it suitable for? Nothing.

Waste not, won't not.

Watch and learn.

Water hole. (Fueling station)

We all die alone.

We all need somebody to lean on.

We always hurt the ones we love.

We are not alone.

We can agree to disagree.

Went from sugar to shit.

Wet backs. (Mexicans)

We want a transparent investigation.

We were born to hear, but we learn to listen.

We will, we will, rock you.

We wish you Love, peace, and soul.

We've come full circle.

What a strangled web we weave when we practice to deceive.

What becomes of the broken hearted?

What begins badly usually ends badly.

Whatchamacallit.

What doesn't kill you makes you stronger.

What doesn't break a man makes a man.

Whatever doesn't kill you makes you stronger.

Whatever you are, be a good one.

What goes around comes back around, nothing stays the same, but GOD.

What goes up must come down.

What is done is done.

What it lies in our power to do, lies in our ability not to do.

What kind of bird can't fly? A jailbird.

What makes you laugh can make you cry.

What makes a good man go bad?

What you see is what you get.

What part of no didn't you understand?

What's black, white, and red all over?

What scares me more is not being remembered.

What's done is done.

What's good for the goose is good for the gander.

What's so good about goodbye?

What's your angle?

What's hers is hers, and what's yours is hers.

What you can't change, stop worrying about it.

When a deal comes across your plate, get a knife and fork.

When in Rome, do like the Romans do.

When it rains, it pours.

When HELL freezes over.

When it's over, it's over.

When life gives you lemons, make lemonade.

When one door closes, another one opens.

When people don't care, they forget what they deserve.

When pigs fly.

When the cat's away, the mice will play.

When the cows come home.

When the legion becomes fact, print the legion.

When the rubber hits the road.

When the shit hits the fan.

When the shit hits the fire.

When there's no clear option, it's best to do nothing.

When there's blood on the streets, buy property.

When there's blood on the streets, someone has to pay.

When the going gets tough, the tough get going.

When you dance to the music, you have to pay the piper.

When you decide to settle for a second, that's what happens to you in life

When you know better, you do better.

When you do what you like to do, you'll never work a day in your life

When you fall, get up and try again.

When you get past the navel, you've got it licked.

When you smile, the whole world smiles with you.

Where do we go from here?

Where there's fire, there's smoke.

Where there's smoke, there's fire.

Where the rubber meets the road.

Where's the beef?

Where words fail, music speaks.

While we're postponing, life speeds up.

Which part of "NO", don't you understand?

White lie.

Whoop de doo.

Will you put that in writing?

Winner takes all.

Winner, winner, chicken dinner.

Winning is not everything but wanting to win is.

Wish in one hand and shit in the other, see which one gets filled the quickest. (Mother)

With friends like you, a hug means I won't pay you back.

Without a shadow of a doubt.

Without Love, you can't survive.

Without people, there's nothing.

Whooo, let the dogs out?

Whoring.

Why do fools fall in Love?

Wolves run in packs.

Women are like missed buses, there'll always be another one.

Women can't do with them and can't do without them.

Women figures that every man that comes along wants them.

Won't bust a grape.

Word.

Word is bond.

Word of mouth is the best advertisement.

Words sure travel fast.

Word to the wise.

Word up.

Working beats waiting.

Wouldn't change it for all the tea in China.

Wouldn't touch you with a ten-foot pole.

Wrong as two left shoes. (Mother)

"Y"

Yes, I said it.

Yesterday is gone, and tomorrow is today.

Yesterday is not ours to recover, but tomorrow is ours to win our loss.

You ain't all day.

You ain't got backbone enough to set up in a chair.

You ain't had none since it had you.

You always want to be in the winner's locker room, not the losers with a towel over your head.

You are a sore loser.

You better ask somebody.

You better check yourself before you wreck yourself.

You better stay low before you catch a halo.

You broke it, you bought it.

You can catch more flies with sugar than with vinegar.

You can do bad by yourself.

You can lead a horse to water, but you can't make him drink.

You can stop a lot of times, but it's not hard to start back. (Drug and alcohol usage)

You can't cross the sea merely by standing and staring at the water.

You can't dodge a bullet.

You can't get blood from a turnip.

You can't have it both ways.

You can't have your cake and eat it too.

You can't judge a book by its cover.

You can't live without GOD.

You can't lose what you never had.

You can't make a rooster stop crowing once the sun rises.

You can't make a whore a housewife.

You can't move forward living in the past.

You can't put a price tag on genius.

You can't stop progress.

You can't take it with you, but ain't nothing wrong with having it while you're here.

You can't teach an old dog new tricks.

You can't win if you don't play.

You can't win them all.

You cooked your goose.

You dig.

You don't pay hookers for sex, you pay them to leave.

You feel me.

You get out what you put in.

You get what you pay for.

You got buzzard luck.

You got life fucked up.

You got more twists than a barrel of pretzels.

You got that right.

You got the energy of the dead.

You got to crawl before you walk.

You got to do what you got to do.

You got to give something to get something.

You have to admit that there's a problem before you can fix it.

You have to be an active recipient in your own life.

You have to be smart to be successful, not ruthless.

You have to crawl before you walk.

You have to do what you have to do.
You have to play the game with the uniform you're issued.
You have to play the hand that you are dealt.
You'll never get rich working on a salary.
You'll never guess.
You'll never hear the shot that kills you.
You miss all the shots you don't take.
You move, you lose.
You never cease to amaze me.
You never fail to amaze me.
You never hear the shot that kills you.
You never miss what you never had.
You never miss your water till your well runs dry.
Young, gifted, and black.
You only live once.
You're a blowhole.
You're an idiot.
You're a player hater.
You're as happy as you choose to be.
You're a wussy.
You're never too smart to learn more.
You're nothing but a fly on the wall.
You're not playing with a full deck.
You're not the sharpest knife in the drawer.
You're out of line.
You're passing off the Pope.
You're shit out of luck.
You're working me like a job.
Your eyes may shine, your teeth my grit, but none of this
    you may not git.

Your hourglass figure.

Your little head should never have control over your big head.

Your mind is shorter than a nats ass. (Mother)

Your mine ain't long as a mustard seed.

You rock.

Your reputation precedes you.

Your smile will give you a positive countenance that will make people feel comfortable around you.

Your word is your bond.

You silly.

You snooze, you lose.

You so crazy.

You so whipped I can spread you on my sandwich.

You take the good with the bad.

You understand me?

You've got to lick it before you stick it.

You've lost your mind. Find it.

You waste, you want. (Mother)

"Z"

Zap it.
Zig Zags. (Papers)
Zip it.

Spiritual sayings and Quotes of the BIBLE

While writing these saying, I encountered the DEVIL's deceitful dealings. He sometimes tried to make me write the wrong quotes and sayings. But I caught the miss prints.

I hope I caught them all.

For years I've wanted to write a book, but I never was able to come up with a subject for the book. I added the Books and Chapters of the Bible for you to reference too.

Preachers, there are some great sermons in these sayings and quotes. Please enjoy. Currently, I am writing another book.

AMEN.

"A"

A bird and a fish can fall in love, but where would they live.
Abortion is MURDER and will be judged by GOD for that.
ABRAHAM lead the first war on EARTH.
Absent in the body, present with the LORD.
Accept CHRIST as LORD and SAVIOR, or you don't know him.
Accept the things you cannot change.
A crisis Christian.
ACTS: 1-8, 1:11. (Light manner)
ACTS: 2:1-4, 2:19-21, 11:14, 15:18, 19:11-17.

ACTS, "Holy Spirit".

Adam named all the species of life.

Adopt the pace of nature, her secret is patience.

A drunk never tells lies.

A father should be smarter than his son.

A GOD of order.

A house divide cannot stand.

All glory and praises go to the LORD GOD.

All men are brothers.

All storms are conquered through prayer.

Always count your blessings.

A man is a thief when he takes something that doesn't belong to him.

A man's guilt is his own grief.

A man has to do what he thinks is right.

A man needs his sons to feel hold.

A man's home is his castle.

A man's tongue is like a shovel, sometimes it can dig his own grave.

A man without the spirit is whipped.

A man who doesn't work ain't respectable.

A man who has wealth will never have enough.

America is corruptive as Sodom and Gomorrah.

Amen!

Am I my brother's keeper? YES.

A mother's love.

An Angel is a created being.

An evil deed hurts the doer more than the victim.

And he said unto to them, go yeah to all the world and preach the gospel.

Angels are assigned to you to protect you. (2 Angels)

Angels are invisible and invincible and do fly.

Angels are turned loose on your enemies.

Angels defeat the wicked on every occasion.

Angels escort you to Heaven when you die.

Angels have superior knowledge, but they don't know the day of the coming of the LORD.

Angels only have a Spirit and a Soul. (No bone are flesh)

Angels watch you intently all the time.

Angels with flaming swords drove Adam and EVE out of the garden of Eden.

Anger is dangerous.

Anger steals your peace and joy.

An idol mind is the Devil's workshop. (Mother)

Anointing is the blessing of what you were gifted to do.

Anti - Christ means the lawless one.

Anything is possible.

Apart from me and GOD, I can do nothing.

A pig is a "hog", little boy.

A prayer of release.

(Archangel) Michael, the Angel of War.

A relaxed attitude leads to a longer life.

Are you your brother's keeper? YES, you are.

A rich man has the chance of getting into Heaven, as a camel has to go thru the eye of a needle.

As a man thinketh, so is He.

As dead as Julius Caesar.

A seed of nothing, quantities a harvest of nothing.

As it was then, so is it now.

Ask, and it shall be given to you.

As often have you done it to the lease of them, you've done it to me.

As the mountains around Jerusalem, so is the LORD around the people of the world.

As the twig is bent, so does the tree.

At the end of time, there will be no more souls in the Halls of Girth and the last birth will be stillborn. (Dead)

A tongue has infected more than a sword.

At the root of every human problem is a sin problem.

A wolf in sheep's clothing.

A woman who fears the LORD should be PRAISED.

"B"

Beauty's only stain deep but hatred always runs through.

Be careful what you say out of your mouth, it will expose you.

Become SEED conscience, not NEED conscience.

Be doers of the word, not only believers of the word.

Be FAITHFUL till death, and I will give you the crown of life.

Behold a pale horse, and the person on it was dead, and HELL followed him.

Behold, I send you out as sheep amidst the wolves.

Being absent in the body is being in the presence of the LORD.

Being in CHRIST is a relationship.

Being over righteous or overwise will destroy you.

Believe that life is worth living and your belief will help create the fact.

Be sure your sins will find you out.

Be thankful for what you got.

Bitterness is anger turned inward, it's destructive.

Black robes in the Judicial system were inducted by Priests.

Blessed are the peacemakers, they will become children of GOD.

Blessed are those who have not seen me but still believe.

Blessed be the name of the LORD.

Blessed he that heareth and doeth.

Blessed is he that listens and doeth, the word of GOD.

Blessed is the man whose sin has been forgiven.

Blood is thicker than water, but the SPIRIT is thicker than blood.

Blood Moons are signs that Jesus is coming soon.

Born again.

Born to be blessed.

Break the shame barrier.

Broad is the way to hell, but narrow is the way to Heaven, from which few will find the way.

Build on the solid rock of life, of JESUS CHRIST.

But if not.

By his stripes, we are healed.

By the authority of JESUS name.

"C"

Can I get a witness?

Case your cares on the LORD because he cares.

Change is the Law of life.

2 CHRONICLES 6:6-7:6.

CHRIST founded Christianity.

CHRIST is still the answer.

Civil disgrace.

Cleanliness is next to GODLINESS.

COLOSSIANS 3:9, 3-11.

Come as you are.

Compromising the Word of GOD is treason in HEAVEN.

Confessing sin is agreeing that you are wrong.

Confessing to GOD is good for the soul.

Conscience is a compass of the soul, so you can determine right from wrong.

Conscience is a river that can not be shut down.

Conscience is the voice of GOD.

Conscience is the word of GOD saying, walk this way.

Conscience of men determines the future of men.

Conscience works from the inside.

2 CORINTHIANS 3:1-3, 10:5.

Counterfeit Christianity.

Count your blessings and be thankful for what you have.

Crucify your WILL and do GOD's WILL.

"D"

Daily renew your mind and attitude.

DANIEL 8:23, 9:25, 12:4.

DAVID killed Goliath.

Death comes soon enough, anyone who hurries it is a damn fool.

Death comes to us all.

Death smiles at us all, and all a man can do is smile back.

DEBT: D=doing, E=everything, B=but, T= tithing.

Defeat is permanent only when you lose hope.

Defeat terrorism by strength, not by compromise.

Defend religious freedom.

Defilement is to make dirty and unclean.

Delayed Obedience is Disobedience.

Deliver us from EVIL ones, demons are very EVIL.

Demons are not fallen angels.

Demons are real.

Demons believe in JESUS, but they don't obey him.

Demons invade you by your invite.

Desperate people do desperate things.

DEUTERONOMY 31:21.

Devine forgiveness demands a change of conduct.

Did you receive the HOLY SPIRIT when you believed?

Disappointment should never lead to disbelief.

Disobedience brings Judgment.

Dispensation of the Holy Spirit.

Doing right ain't got no end.

Don't be afraid of the HOLY SPIRIT.

Don't be caught dead without JESUS.

Don't be caught dead without JESUS.

Don't die a cheap copy of someone else.

Don't ever give up on your FAITH.

Don't expect life to be fair.

Don't go around saying that life owes you something, it was here first.

Don't let disappointment lead you to disbelief.

Don't let the fear of what you don't have, stop you from walking into the blessings of what God has for you.

Don't live your life looking through the rearview mirror.

Don't loose FAITH when you have to endure.

Don't marry an unbeliever.

Don't pray when it rains if you don't pray when the sun shines.

Don't quit, move on.

Don't take GOD's meekness for weakness.

Don't take life too seriously, you'll never get out alive.

Don't throw stones.

Doubting Thomas, the Disciple.

Do unto others as you would have them do unto you.

Dream big.

During the tribulation, GOD is going to release his Angels to kill over 1/3 of all the population on Earth, the Ungodly.

"E"

ECCLESIATES 4:9, 8:16.

Eden is a place of pleasure and delight.

Eight (8) is the number of new beginnings in the BIBLE. ELOHIM, the mighty GOD of ISREAL. (The Almighty GOD)

Endure, and GOD will make a away.

Endure to the end, fight till the end.

Enter his gates with thanksgiving and his courts with praise.

Even in the darkest of night, there's hope.

Even while in HEAVEN, you can be cast out. Don't be a second LUCIFER.

Every good and perfect gift comes from GOD.

Every knee shall bow, every tongue shall confess that He is LORD.

Every miracle has two parts, yours and GOD'S.

Everyone wants to go to Heaven, but no one wants to die.

Every silver lining has a cloud.

Everything good came from a day of trouble.

Everything is impossible till someone does it.

Everythings is going to be alright.

Everything that GOD controls GIVES.

Everything that happens to you happens for you.

Everything we have, we lose.

EXODUS 20:16, 2:21, 23:20-23.

Eyes have not seen nor ears have heard what GOD has for us in Heaven.

Eyes, the window to the soul.

EZEKIEL 8:12.

EZEKIEL 38, 39, 46.

"F"

FACTS don't change our lives, friendship changes our lives.

FAITH is always tested by fire.

FAITH is being sure of what we hope for.

FAITH is how you exercise the grace that God gives you to grow.

FAITH is the action with God, it motivates us to do the right thing.

FAITH is the confident conviction that GOD will do what he said he would do.

FAITH is the opposite of fear and fear is the opposite of FAITH.

FAITH is the overcoming of doubt.

FAITH is the victory that overcomes the world.

FAITH is when you believe in GOD when you can't hear him speak.

FAITH leads to patience and patience leads to the promise of GOD.

FAITH until death.

FAITH won't work until you do.

False knowledge is more dangerous than ignorance.

Fear is, the action without GOD, it motivates us to do the wrong thing. Fear is your worst enemy.

Fear the LORD and turn away from EVIL.

Fear not, be of good cheer.

Fear of the LORD is the beginning of all WISDOM.

Fiery trials are normal.

Fight the good fight.

Fill your children with the GOSPEL of GOD.

Find a prayer partner.

Find a verse and live on it.

First Heaven is the Sun, Moon, and the Stars.

Fix your eyes on JESUS, he will never leave you.

Flying saucer and extraterrestrials are real.

For every way of living, something has to be given up.

Forgive and forget.

Forgive as GOD forgave you.

Forgiveness is a fresh start.

Forgiveness is a full pardon, it unlocks the door of resentment.

Forgiveness is essential for your health.

Forgiveness is not given, it's earned.

Forgiveness liberates.

Forgive others.

Forgive our debtors.

Forgive them, for they know not what they do.

Forgive totally.

Forgive your enemies, but don't forget their names.

For GOD'S sake.

For GOD so loved the world that he gave his only begotten son that whosoever believeth in him should not perish but have everlasting life. (ST JOHN 3:16)

For goodness sake.

For Heaven's sake.

For he who the LORD sets free, is free indeed.

For Pete's sake.

For thine is the kingdom without end.

*For those who call upon the name of the LORD, shall be
saved.*

For whom the bells tow, they tow for thee.

For whom the LORD sets free is free indeed.

Four BLOOD MOONS, JOEL 2: ACTS 2:19-21.

Freedom is the responsibility to do what we want.

Free from the world, the flesh, and the DEVIL.

From the bottom, there's no way but UP.

"G"

GENESIS 3:8, 11:7.

GENESIS is the first book of the BIBLE.

George Muller came to live by Faith. (Helped orphans)

Get all you can and can all you get.

Get into GOD'S presents with praise.

Get over it and press on.

Get your eyes off what you don't have.

Giver's gain.

Give thanks to the Lord for his loving-kindness is everlasting.

Give the DEVIL his due.

Give the LORD praise and glory.

Giving, opens the way to receiving.

GOD answers pacific prayers.

GOD bless the child that's got his own.

GOD can bring you through the fire without the smell of smoke.

GOD cannot answer your prayers until you pray about it.

GOD cannot be in the presents of EVIL.

GOD cannot hear prayers from an unforgiving husband or wife.

GOD can not lie.

GOD cannot remember sin that has been washed in the blood of JESUS.

GOD cannot worship because there's nothing higher than the highest. (GOD)

GOD created the HEAVENS and the EARTH.

GOD delights in the prosperity and progress of his children.

GOD designed the Prayer Shawl.

GOD did not respect CAIN. No blood offering.

GOD does not approve of same-sex marriages, if so then he would have to apologize to Solomon.

GOD does not hear prayers from an unforgiving husband or wife.

GOD does not make EVIL people, they make themselves.

GOD does not only judge nations, but HE judges individuals also.

GOD doesn't get old because he was from the beginning.

GOD doesn't get wiser because he knew everything from the end to the beginning. GOD doesn't like ugly.

GOD doesn't only judge nations, but HE also judges individuals.

GOD doesn't remember sin that has been washed in the blood of JESUS.

GOD don't like ugly.

GOD gave Noah the rainbow sign, said no more water, the FIRE NEXT TIME.

GOD gives seeds to sowers and harvests to receivers.

GOD gives the best of things in the worst of times.

God gives you the problems.

GOD gives you wisdom.

GOD has a set time for everything.

GOD has a zero-tolerance for sin.

GOD has (8) eight names.

GOD has done for us what we cannot do for ourselves.

GOD has your name, and the DEVIL has your number.

GOD is able to provide, he's just looking for someone to do it for.

GOD is absolutely in control of the Earth.

GOD is a friend that sticketh closer than a brother.

GOD is a GOD of second chances and new beginnings.

GOD is BIG, sin is small.

GOD is going to release Micheal, Gabriel, and his Angles to kill 1/4 of the world's population.

GOD is good, ALL THE TIME.

GOD is greater than your failure.

GOD is LOVE.

GOD is obligated and bound by his word.

GOD is still the master of the storm.

GOD is supernatural.

GOD is the architect of the ages.

GOD is the founder of the University of Adversity.

GOD is the same yesterday, today, and tomorrow.

GOD is too loving to be unkind, too perfect to make a mistake.

GOD is with us.

GOD keeps his word for a thousand years.

GOD knows the end from the beginning.

GOD likes improvement.

GOD loves a cheerful giver.

GOD makes no mistakes.

GOD never changes.

GOD never lies.

GOD never takes something from you unless he's going to give you something better.GOD resists the pride and gives grace to the humble.

GOD. (No sound, no light, and no distractions)

GOD only asks for help from those who can give it.

GOD requires a physical reaction. (Fasting)

GOD resists the pride and gives grace to the humble.

GOD said that he would not put the deceases that he put on the Egyptians on us. GOD save the Queen.

GOD's delays are not GOD's denials.

GOD shall conquer EVIL.

GOD's love is unconditional.

GOD's never late.

GOD so loved the world that he gave his only begotten son.

GOD's Speed.

GOD's stress remover is solitude.

GOD takes care of babies and fools.

GOD thinks in man.

GOD wants us to be with him for a relationship.

GOD will never leave or forsake you.

GOD wills you the desires of your heart.

Good neighbors come in all colors.

Good things come to those who wait.

Go to somewhere in your home where there are no distractions to be along with Grace is given in spite of our sins.

Greater is he who is in us that is in the world.

Great trial brings great triumph.

Growth is the only evidence of Life.

Guilt is real because sin is real.

"H"

Habitually seeking and setting your mind towards CHRIST.

Hallelujah to the Lamb of GOD.

Hate imagines revenge.

Have FAITH in GOD, and ALL things are possible.

Have FAITH in the word of GOD.

Heap sees and few know.

Hear today, gone tomorrow.

HEAVEN and HELL are for real.

HEAVEN must be missing an angel.

HEAVENS right here on Earth.

Heavy is the head that wears the crown.

HEBREWS 2:3, 7:25, 10:8, 12:22, 13:5.

He created us to reveal his love, good, provisions, kindness, etc.

He has RISEN.

He holds the seven seas in the palms of his hands.

He is a friend that sticketh closer than a brother.

HE is the ALPHA and the OMEGA, the first and the last.

HE is the CREATOR.

HE knows the END to the BEGINNING.

Helen Keller always knew that GOD was there, she just never knew what his name was.

Hell, or high water.

Helping others makes the strength of ten.

He that believes in CHRIST is ALIVE, and those who don't believe are DEAD.

He that believeth in me shall never die.

He that heareth and doeth my word is my Disciple.

He that heareth and doeth my word is my Disciple.

He that keepeth Israel neither slumbers are sleep.

HE that winneth souls are Wise.

HELL has no fury like a woman scorned.

HELL, is the punishment for sin.

He's my right-hand man.

He's, the defender of ISREAL who neither slumbers nor sleep.

He's the light of the world.

He who cannot forgive breaks the bridge for which he has to cross.

He who does not LOVE does not know GOD.

He whoever calls on the LORD shall be forgiven.

He who maketh haste to become rich will not be innocent.

He who takes up the sword will perish by the sword.

He who winneth souls are wise.

He who wins souls is wise.

Holly molly.

Honor thy mother and thy father and thy days on Earth will be longer.

Hope is proof of the presence of GOD in your Life. Hope thou in GOD.

HOSEA 2:15.

How you look is not what you are.

Hurting people hurts people.

Husbands love your wives as JESUS loved the Church.

"I"

I am a sinner in need a savior.

I am my brother's keeper.

I am the TRUTH and the LIGHT sayeth the LORD.

Icicles in Church come from popsicles. (Fathers)

Idol mind is the DEVIL'S workshop.

If a man lack knowledge, let him ask for it.

If any man comes after me, let him deny himself.

If GOD agreed to homosexuality, he would have to apologize to Sodom and Gomorrah.

If GOD didn't want them sheared, he wouldn't have made them sheep.

If GOD is for you, who can be against you.

If GOD is in it, there's no limit.

If GOD'S willing.

If it had been a snake, it would have bit you.

If something makes you hate the Jewish people, it's Demonic.

If the foundation is destroyed, what can America do?

If you are not an eyewitness, you are a false witness.

If you are truly saved, you will not feel comfortable in sin.

If you ask for GOD to forgive you, he will do it.

If you can't control what's defeating you, then what's defeating you will control you.

If you can't say something good about someone, don't say anything at all.

If you can't trust GOD, you can't trust know one.

If you confess with your mouth and believe in your heart that JESUS is LORD, you shall be saved.

If you don't believe in Miracles, you will when you need one.

If you don't have anything good to say, say nothing.

If you don't know JESUS CHRIST, you are a slave to sin.

If you don't like going to GOD'S house, what makes you think he's going to let you in his house?

If you don't use your freedom to defend your freedom, you will lose your freedom.

If you plant something, you reap something. (Anything)

If you're not an eyewitness, you are a false witness.

If you're not looking for the coming of Christ, then you're not going with him when he comes.

If you're out for revenge, dig two graves.

If you see a need and you pray for it, Mercy is doing something about it.

If you take one step, he'll take two.

If you tell the truth all the time, you don't have to have a good memory.

If you want something done right, do it yourself.

If you waste, you'll want. (Mother)

I have a dream. (MLK)

Imagination is the foresight of a destination.

Imagination is the hidden force of destiny and potential.

I'm equal to anything through CHRIST.

I'm in Heaven.

In a heartbeat.

Information without application leads to frustration.

IN GOD, WE TRUST.

In HEAVEN, memories are grateful to people.

In HELL Memories torment people. (They'll be out of the grace of GOD.)

In JESUS's name, Amen.

In Life, you have to take the bitter with the sweet.

In quietness shall be your strength.

Inside all older persons is a younger person saying what happened.

Inspiration without information leads to frustration.

Intelligence is used for the goodness of mankind.

In the kingdom of Heaven, NOTHING JUST HAPPENS.

In the very best of men, there's a little bad and in the worst of men, there's a little good.

In war, there is no substitute for Victory.

In wine, there's truth.

Iron sharpens iron.

ISAIAH 10:27, 28:7, 30:15, 45:11, 62:1, 88:8.

I serve no other GOD, but the GOD of Abraham.

Isreal is the future of the world.

Isreal, Prince with GOD.

Is it all part of a master plan?

I swear before GOD.

I swear to GOD.

I take everything you say as gospel.

It always rains before the rainbow.

It does not lack faith when you ask GOD, why?

It doesn't take much FAITH to believe in a GOD who has never fail.

It is the LORD who gives you the Power of wealth.

It never pays to even the odds.

It rains on the Just and the Unjust.

It takes a village to raise a child.

It's a lot easier to ask forgiveness than permission.

It's always darkest before the storm.

It's a miracle.

It's better to be a lion for a day than a sheep all your Life.

It's better to give than to receive.

It's GOD's job to judge, the job of the holy spirit is to convict and our job to love. It's GOD's will for you to prosper.

It's harvest time.

It's impossible to govern America without the Bible. (George Washington)

It's my cross to bear.

It's never right to do the wrong thing.

It's never too late to make the right choices.

It's not what you believe, it's what you obey. (The word of GOD)

It's not what you eat but what's eating you.

It's only by the grace of God that I'm alive.

It's possible to govern our nation without the Power of GOD.

It's seed time.

It's the calm before the storm.

It's the LORD who gives you the Power of wealth.

It's the obedience to GOD that matters.

I will bless those who bless you and curse those who curse you.

I will destroy all nations that come against Jerusalem.

I won't tell you anything wrong. (Mother)

"J"

JACOB means heel holder, he held Angel's heel and demanded it to bless himn before it returned to Heaven.

JAMES 2:19, 3:5-8, 4:5, 2:19.

Jealousy is a disease of the flesh.

JEREMIAH 6:16.

Jerusalem, DC = David's City.

Jerusalem does not occupy the land, they OWN the land.

Jerusalem is the Epic Center of the world.

Jerusalem is the undivided country of Israel.

Jerusalem the city of GOD.

JESUS and John the Baptist were cousins.

JESUS came to Earth to crush the head of the DEVIL.

JESUS CHRIST comes to restore us for what we lost in the garden of EDEN.

JESUS CHRIST comes to save those who were lost.

JESUS CHRIST is still the reason for Christmas.

JESUS didn't teach his disciples to preach but how to Pray.

JESUS had other brothers who did not believe in him. They hid from him.

JESUS is the beginning of GOD's creation.

JESUS is the reason for the season.

JESUS knows the worst about you and the best about you.

JESUS led the war in HEAVEN.

JESUS never sent his disciples out to preach without teaching them how to defeat Demons.

JESUS rose on Sunday, First Fruits.

JESUS said, don't believe in man but in me.

JESUS said, forgive immediately.

JESUS said I am the living water, seek me, and you'll never trust.

JESUS said, you're either for me or against me.

JESUS satisfies our souls.

JESUS was called an Angel of the LORD, as he ascended to heaven.

JESUS wept.

JESUS will rule with a rod of iron when he return.

Jewish people don't occupy Isreal, they own it.

JOEL 2-3, the four Blood Moons.

JOHN 1 1:9 Believers should remember this verse.

JOHN 3:16, 4:3, 5:20, 6:9-14, 6:21, 10:10, 14:2 & 3, 15:5, 19:30.

JOHN the Baptist and JESUS CHRIST were cousins.

JOHN took care of MARY after JESUS died.

Joy comes in the morning.

Joy to the world the LORD has come. Let Earth receive her KING.

Juda is where the word Jew comes from.

Judged by your friends.

Judge, not yet he is not judge.

Jump the broom.

JUST DO IT. The will of GOD.

JUSTICE IS BLIND.

"K"

Keep seeking GOD's word.

Keep the FAITH.

Keep worshiping GOD, regardless.

Kindness is loving those who hate you.

1 KINGS 17:8-16.

2 KINGS 2:9,11, 19:14.

Knock, and the door shall be opened.

Knowing the LORD and following him are two different things.

Knowing what to do is just as important as knowing what not to do.

Knowing without doing is like farming without planting.

Knowledge is Power, never stop learning.

"L"

Laying on the hands.

Lean not unto your own understanding, but trust in the LORD with ALL your heart.

Learn to live with your conscience.

Leopards can't they're spots.

Let go and let GOD.

Let no man deceive you, said JESUS CHRIST.

Let no man take your Joy from you.

Let there be light, and there was light.

Let your mouth be ruled by the Law of Kindness.

Life comes at you quickly.

Life divine intervention.

Life is about choices, and you are responsible for your choices Life is about making hard choices.

Life is a good fight of FAITH.

Life is a marathon, not a dash. Run to win.

Life is a school.

Life is love, and love is Life.

Life is not measured by the things we don't have.

Life is short.

Life is the sum of our choices.

Life is what you make it.

Life moves in one direction, move with it.

Light conquers darkness.

Live and let live.

Live by the gun, die by the gun.

Live by the sword, die by the sword.

Live, laugh, and be happy, the best is yet to come.

Look, and you shall be found.

Look to the hills from which my strength comes.

Look up, pack up, we're going up in the twinkling of an eye.

LOVE at first sight.

LOVE does not worship other GODS.

LOVE is imperative in the word of GOD.

LOVE is not envy, LOVE does not boost.

LOVE is not what you say, it's what you do.

LOVE is patient.

LOVE one another as I have LOVED you. (JESUS to the Disciples)

LOVE people, not things.

LOVE thy enemies.

LOVE thy neighbor.

LOVE your wives as CHRIST loved the Church.

LUKE 1:26-38, 6:26-35, 8:28, 9:23, 11:21 & 22, 19:42, 21:24, 21:27-28, 22:61&62, 24:1-8, 24:44-49, 26-35.

Lust, Rust, and Dust are the three sections of marriage.

"M"

Make failure your teacher.

Make GOD first in your Life.

Man cannot live by bread alone.

Man was cursed to work, and women were cursed to have babies.

MARK 1:39, 5:41, 6:45-56, 13:32.

MARK 15-17, The Great Commissions.

MATTHEW 1:39, 6:12-13, 6:9-13, 10:21, 12:25-26, 12:29, 16 & 17, 24:1 & 2, 25:40, 27:4-9, 28:9, 16.

May you be in Heaven a half hour before the devil knows you're gone.

May you live as long as you want and never want as long as you live.

Meditate on the word of CHRIST, do it over and over in your mind.

Meditation is the soul's perspective glass.

Men and women are not always right, but GOD'S word is always right.

Mental philosophy and knowledge cannot change the heart, only JESUS can change the heart.

Miracles happen at the time of the storm.

Misery is an obsession.

Mistakes never drive GOD away.

Money is the root of ALL evil.

MOSES wrote the first five books of the Bible.

Most of the time, we don't see the answer when it's already in your hands.

"N"

Negotiate, demonstrate, resist.

Never bow down to bitterness, let it go.

Never put off tomorrow what you can do today.

No death to the believers.

No man can escape his conscience.

No man is a failure who has friends.

No man is an island.

No man knoweth the time or the day.

No master is greater than his servant.

None violence.

No one escapes stormy weather.

No one knows the day is the hour of your coming.

No other GOD but the God of Abraham, Issac, and Jacob.

No parent should have to bury their child.

No parent should ever have to live passed their child.

No peace for those who don't know JESUS as LORD and Savior.

No peace to the wicked sayeth the LORD.

No religion is responsible for terrorism, people are responsible for terrorism. No rest for the wicked.

No taller than tits high to a puppy dog.

Not believing that Jesus died for our sin, one chooses to die in his own sin. Nothing has meaning till we give it meaning.

Nothing in Life is free.

Nothing is impossible for those that believe.

Nothing is impossible with GOD.

Nothing that ever happens to you is ever wasted.

Not one of us is righteous.

Not only do you have to have religious roots, but also, spiritual roots.

No way to go but up.

No weapons formed against you shall prosper.

"O"

OBADIAH 1:15.

Obedience brings blessings.

Obedience is better than sacrifice.

Obey GOD's LAW & seek him with ALL thy HEART.

Obey your mother and father, honor them when they are gone.

OMG.

Once a thief, always a thief.

Once spoken, it cannot be taken away. (A blessing)

One day at a time.

One of the greatest fears in my Life is to believe in a lie.

Only GOD can multiply what you have.

Only GOD is the CONQUEROR of Death, Hell, and the Grave.

Only in the storms of battles will you discover how great GOD is.

Only the dead are without fear.

On PASSOVER, when you come in one door, you must go out the opposite.

On this rock, I build my Church, and the gates of hell shall not destroy it.

Open his word in order to focus on him.

Optimism is the foundation key to all Success.

Our daily bread.

Our God is able.

Our Life is what our thoughts make it.

Ours is not to do are die, ours is but to reason why.

Our yearning will always endure our earnings.

Out of the mouth speaks things of the heart.
Out of your pain can come your purpose.

"P"

Paradise and Heaven is the same place, The Third Heaven.

Pass me not O' Gentle Savior.

Patience is a virtue.

Patience is the companion of wisdom.

Patience is the willingness to wait.

PAUL said to beware of dogs.

PAUL wrote most of the New Testament.

PAUL wrote over one-third of the BIBLE.

Pay your Tithe where you're spiritually feeding.

Peace is the fruit of repentance.

Peace is the fruit of righteousness.

Peace is the gift of GOD.

Peace is the opposite of hatred.

Peace on Earth to those who GOD approves.

People in HELL want ice water but you don't always get what you want.

People that talk to people about others will talk to other people about you.

People under the influence stand out.

Perfect LOVE cast out fear.

Pergamum city is where Satin lives.

Pluralism is serving more than one GOD but not JESUS.

Power without the characteristics to control that Power is the formula for the end of the world.

Practice what you preach.

Praise GOD daily, it keeps the DEVIL from entering your mind.

Praise GOD for his goodness.

Praise GOD in times of trouble.
Praise is an act of your will.
Praise the LORD.
Praise the LORD with your whole heart.
Praising GOD removes all anxiety.
Praising JESUS releases the supernatural power of GOD.
Pray.
Prayer builds confidence.
Prayer gets you ready to do GOD's will.
Prayer is the pathway to GOD.
Prayers are like incense that makes things better and sweet.
Prayer should be your first choice, not your last chance.
Pray for those who despitefully use you.
Pray, Praise and Power.
Praying indicates physical and spiritual needs.
Preaching should be more than Life changing, but Life rearranging.
Prepare for war in a time of peace. (Mother)
Pretense in prayer can stop you from hearing from GOD.
Price can never be placed on friendship.
Pride causes spiritual blindness.
Pride consumes everything it touches.
Pride goes before destruction.
Principles of us are to work hard.
Problems are nothing more than resistance.
PROVERBS 6:18, 6-21.
PSALM 2:4, 50:15, 63:1-6, 100:4, 150:15, 119:9.
Publicly profess your FAITH in CHRIST.
Pure as the driven snow.

Put in front of you what you love are what you don't will destroy you.

Put on a garment of praise for the spirit of heaveness.

Put um in the LORD's hands. (Mother)

"Q"

Quick success is not lasting success.
Quitting is beneath the dignity of a child of GOD.

"R"

Rabbi Judah Ben Samuel (prophecy) said that GOD has divided time into 50-year Jubilees.

Rationalization of sin is the DEVILS way to dispute the word of GOD.

Read the BIBLE and be loyal to the Word of God, you can't know the BIBLE without reading it.

Real accomplishments in Life begin with FAITH.

Real Power is patience.

Reject the DEVIL, and he will retreat from you.

Rejoice, Rejoice, Rejoice.

Rejoice, your redemption draweth nigh.

Religion always scratches where the body doesn't itch.

Remember the sabbath day and keep it holy.

Repentance is about a change of Life.

Repentance is turning my back on sin and walking with GOD.

Repent your sins.

Represent the LOVE of JESUS.

Respect is earned, not demanded.

Respect is one of the most important things in Life.

Respect your elders.

Respect your mother and father, and your days will be longer.

Rest in Peace.

Resurrection Sunday.

Returning the church to the book of ACTS.

REVELATIONS 5:11, 9:15, 12:10, 13:16, 14:19-20, 19:10, 19:19-20.

Revenge is a meal best served cold.
Revenge is mine sayeth the LORD.
Right always outweighs wrong.
Right as rain.
Right follows right.
Rocky is the road to marriage.
ROMANS 1:21, 8:7, 8:28, 12:2.

"S"

Salvation comes from the Jews.

Salvation is amongst the Jews.

2 SAMUEL 14:40.

SATAN comes in sheep clothing.

SATAN comes to destroy and kill.

SATAN hates the BIBLE and fears the blood of the cross.

SATAN is a defeated foe.

Saying the right thing at the right time is priceless.

Say, Thy Will Be Done and do it (the will of GOD), and you'll reach your highest potential.

Second Heaven is the Mid Heaven. (The DEVIL'S domain)

Security and happiness cannot be bought.

Seeing is believing.

Seek, and you shall find, ask, and the door shall be open unto you.

Self-control is the ability to make yourself do what it doesn't want to. Selfishness is spiritual cancer.

Self-preservation is the first law of nature.

Serious than a deacon.

Service is your well-earned ticket to HEAVEN.

Set your mind on GOD for instant encouragement.

Seven is GOD's perfect number.

SHALOM = PEACE.

Sickness comes into the body from resentment and unforgiveness.

Sin is a separator.

Sin is rebellion, not a mistake.

Sin is those who knoweth and doeth not.

Sin separates man from GOD because he is holly.

Solitude helps protect your health.

Solitude helps to face the day.

Solitude strips us from all our pride.

Some people go to church all their lives and still don't know GOD.

Sometimes the way you feel affects the way you act.

Sometimes you have to listen to the wisdom of a child.

Sometimes your religion gets in the way of submitting your relationship with CHRIST.

Spare the rod or belt, spoil the child.

Speak of the Devil.

Stay away from the UNGODLY.

Stealing is when you don't BELIEVE that GOD will provide for you.

Stop blaming others for what you have done.

Stop comparing yourselves amongst yourselves.

Stop giving for a favor.

Stop living your Life looking through the rearview window.

Stop praying for great and wonderful things if you're not ready for greater STORMS.

Stop worrying about what you're not and be happy with what you are.

Strength can be a weakness for some people.

Stretching the blanket, a little. (The truth)

Stubbornness is adultery.

Submission is how you accomplish the mission.

Success is a choice based on GOD's will or wisdom.

Suffering is fuel for the soul.

Suffering is one of GOD's primary training tools for his people.

"T"

Take charge of your life or someone else will.

Take up your cross and follow me.

Teamwork makes the dream work.

Tell the truth and shame the Devil.

The Alpha and the Omega, the first and the last. GOD and JESUS Christ.

The Antichrist: By peace, he will destroy many.

The Antichrist comes after the Rapture.

The Antichrist is here on earth, NOW.

The Anti-Christ will be a Gentile and a man of war.

The apple of GOD's eye. (The Jewish People)

The Ark of the covenant held the Ten Commandments also, the Rams Horns, that when blown, brought down the walls of Jericho by sound.

The basic word of Natural Law is the BIBLE.

The best of times is the end of times.

The best proof of Love is trust.

The BIBLE can restore (7) times what the DEVIL has taken.

The BIBLE entails the mind of GOD.

The BIBLE is a book of transformation not just information.

The BIBLE is evidence of Life after Death.

The BIBLE is so simple that a fool can air in.

The BIBLE is the book that reads you, you don't read it.

The BIBLE is the compass of the soul.

The BIBLE teaches from GENESIS to REVELATIONS that givers gain.

The bigger the lie, the more people will believe it.

The biggest room in the world is the room for improvement.

The blood, the water, and the oil. (Baptism)

The borrower is SLAVE to the LENDER. (Prov. 22:7)

The church is not a retirement center for the elderly but a recruiting center for the LORD your GOD.

The cure for America is preaching and practicing the BIBLE.

The darkest of your days could be your brightest. (Mother)

The day will come that all you have is what you've given to GOD.

The dead are quickly forgotten.

The Death and resurrection of Jesus Christ bought us salvation.

The debtor is a slave to the lender.

The DEVIL always strikes at the weakest points, the children.

The DEVIL is a lie.

The DEVIL is in the details.

The DEVIL is the master of deception.

The DEVIL knows that the Bible is true.

The DEVIL made me do it.

The DEVIL's disciples.

The DEVIL's shadow.

The difference between a piece of coal and a diamond is the trouble it endured.

The doctrinaire of Demons says that you don't have to repent or confess your sins because you're already going to Heaven. It also teaches the way to Heaven without JESUS. (Impossible)

The door of happiness is locked without Mercy.

The doors of wisdom are never shut.

The earth is the LORD's and all the things within.

The effort of FAITH is your effort, the outcome is GOD's.

The end justifies the means.

The End of Days.

The essence of FAITH is that GOD is with you RIGHT NOW.

The essence of tranquility.

The EVIL toddler to the slaughter.

The fact that you don't believe that JESUS is coming, means that he is coming.

The FATHER, (GOD) doesn't know what the flesh feels, but JESUS does.

The fear of the LORD is the beginning of WISDOM.

The fight for human rights is not a spectator sport, but a participatory sport. (Dick Gregory)

The first HEAVEN is where the sun, moon, stars and clouds are.

The first shall be last, and the last shall be first.

The first thing that's given to you when you enter the world and the last thing that's remembered is your NAME.

The flesh is weak.

The flowers may whittle, the grass may fade, but the word of GOD lasts forever.

The foolish shall confound the wise.

The fruit of the spirit is LOVE.

The GOD of Abraham, that's who I serve.

The GOD we serve is a GOD of Miracles.

The Golden Rule.

The greater the failure the greater GOD's grace.

The greater the problem the greater the promise.

The greater your mission, the greater the storm.

The greatest among you is the servants of all.

The greatest commandment is to LOVE your neighbor as yourself.

The greatest gift in Life is to be remembered.

The greatest trick that the DEVIL ever played was to convince the world that he didn't exist.

The Greeks named the days of the week after the sun, moon, and five known planets, in turn, named after the gods Ares, Hermes, Zeus, Aphrodite and Cronus. (The days of the Gods)

The hand that rocks the cradle is the hand that rules the world. (Abraham Lincoln)

The happiest people in the world are the people who live in the word of GOD.

The head of every woman is a MAN, the head of every MAN is CHRIST.

The heart of a fool is in his mouth.

The Holy Grail.

The Holy Spirit draws you to CHRIST.

The Holy Spirit is a hovering force that brings Power over us. The purpose is to testify the Power of the LORD, to bring unity to the body of CHRIST (Church), it teaches what to say when you don't know what to say, and to bring you, LOVE.

The Holy Spirit is the visible presence of GOD in us. He displaces the Spirit of God in us.

The Holy Spirit is the third person of the Trinity.

The increase of sacrifice is the increase of GOD's favor.

The Jewish people DO NOT occupy but OWN the land of Israel.

The juice of courage. (Alcohol)

The KING is coming, the KING is coming, the KING is coming and all his GLORY.

The KING of Kings and LORD of LORDS.

The LAMBS book of LIFE. Your name must appear.

The language in HEAVEN is Hebrew.

The Lassoed lightning.

The last shall be first, and the first shall be last.

The lesser of two EVILS.

The less you talk, the more you're listened to.

The light of the world, JESUS CHRIST.

The LORD delights in the prosperity of the believers.

The LORD doesn't like ugly.

The LORD giveth and the LORD taketh away, blesseth be the name of the LORD.

The LORD is my shepherd, I shall not want.

The LORD is my Strength, for whom should I be afraid.

The LORD is never late. (Mother)

The LORD is the answer.

The LORD is the LORD of all, if not, he's not LORD at all.

The LORD loves a cheerful giver.

The LORD moves in mysterious ways.

The LORD works in mysterious ways, his will be done.

The LORD works in number 1-7 days and first-twelfth month.

The Love of money is the root of all EVIL.

The man who does not forgive, breaks the bridge that he must cross.

The man who does not work doesn't eat.

The mark of the beast. (666)

The meek shall inherit the earth.

The mind of men is at war with the mind of GOD.

The Miracle of Salvation is the greatest Miracle you can see.

The more money you make, the more problems you make.

The most troubling churches are churches without trouble.

The ones that are the closest to you are the ones that give you the most trouble.

The ones who are for you are greater than the ones who are against you.

The one who has saved one Life has changed the world.

The one who submits his will to CHRIST will be saved.

The only true wisdom is in knowing you know nothing.

The path to GOD has many directions but the same destination.

The penalty of sin is Death.

The people came to see JESUS because they wanted to see Power.

The Permissive Will of GOD is what GOD permits you to do.

The person who can bring the spirit of laughter into a room is indeed blessed.

The person who looks up to GOD doesn't look down on anyone.

THE POWER OF GIVING, PRAYER, and FORGIVING.

The Power of Life and Death is in the tongue.

The Power of two.

The prayer of release. (Asking GOD to take the suffering from this world.)

The Prayer Shaw was designed by GOD himself.

The price of world peace is world righteousness.

The Prince of Darkness, Satin, and the Devil.

The Prince of Peace. (JESUS CHRIST)

The Prodigal son left home as a rich man and came back looking like a slave.

The provisions of GOD is in the promises of GOD.

The purpose of Angels is to worship GOD.

The quality of the house is determined by the quality of the storm.

The quiet before the storm.

The rainbows are there to remind you of the water destruction of the earth.

The Rapture.

There are limits to what a man will do for money but no limits to what he will do for Love.

There are not days of miracles but a GOD of Miracles.

There are not many roads to Heaven, just one.

There are no such thing as ordinary people, just people who do unordinary things.

There are only two choices in Life, GOOD and BAD.

There are two kinds of people in the world: the takers and the givers.

The takers may eat better, but the givers sleep better.

There are two sides to every story: somewhere in the middle lies the TRUTH.

The reason for the lights on your Christmas trees indicates that JESUS is the light of the world.

There is a DEVIL.

There is no distance in prayer.

There is no other GOD's beside thee.

There is no peace for non-believers.

There is no right in the wrong.

There is nothing impossible with GOD.

There is no wealth but Life.

There is redemption for ALL.

The rejection of GOD is the biggest ingratitude of appreciation of GOD's grace.

There's a season for all times.

There's a thousand reason for failure, but only one to be successful.

There's just one GOD, the GOD of Abraham, Isaac, and Jacob.

There's more than one way to skin a cat.

There's no saying "Have a nice day in Heaven." It's always a great day in Heaven.

There's nothing that you can do to disqualify yourself from GOD'S Love.

There's nothing wrong in the world, but wrong WILL.

There's only one DEVIL but many DEMONS.

There's pleasure in sex for a season.

There's Power in prayer. (Thank you, atheist, for recognizing that.)

The resurrection means that SATAN is a defeated foe.

There was a third of the angels in Heaven that was casted out with the DEVIL.

There were 8 transitions at the cross.

There will be signs in the SUN, MOON, and the STARS.

The righteous are as bold as a lion.

The road to Heaven is narrow, which few will find.

The road to Hell is wide. Many choose this way.

The robin got his red breast from bathing in the blood pools of the crucified JESUS CHRIST.

The rod of God was Mose's staff.

The salt of the earth.

The scum of the earth.

The second HEAVEN is where the DEVIL resides.

The second reason for the crucifixion is the WORK IS DONE.

The secret of Life, you just hang around till you get used to it.

The sins of the father is inherited by the sons.

The sins of the father will often be visited upon the children.

The sky is GOD's billboard of signs in the heavens.

The spirit of Akins takes from GOD.

The spoken words of GOD are a two-edged sword.

The stone was not rolled away so JESUS could get out, but for us to get in.

The storm isn't sent to you by choice but to determine your destiny.

The Strength of a family is like the Strength of an army and loyalty.

The SUN and MOON are GOD's special agents.

The sweetest sound is that of the woman we love.

The sword of the truth is the word of GOD. (The BIBLE)

The third Heaven is where JESUS sits on the right hand of GOD. (PARADISE)

The Tithe is not a debt we owe but a seed we sow.

The truth hurts.

The truth is not for all men but only for those who seek it.

The truth is what GOD's Word says it is.

The truth shall set you free.

The truth will set you free.

The universe doesn't always solve the problem, but it should.

The universe is the only thing that's bigger than yourself.

The unseen is greater than the seen.

The UPPER ROOM.

The venom of a jealous woman is more dangerous than a venomous snake.

The wage of sin is Death.

The ways of the LORD are beyond understanding.

The when and then will curse you.

The WILL of GOD is what GOD expects you to do.

The whole world is a stage, and everybody plays a part.

The Word and Will of GOD are synonymous.

The word of God lasts forever.

The world is your oyster.

The worst thing an honest man can do, is to make an honest mistake.

The wrong will be righted.

The young are truthful.

They that have, not LOVE, have not GOD.

Things that are not seen are greater than things that are seen.

Things that can be taken to the grave are your word and honor.

Think of changing yourself before changing the world.

This is the day the LORD has made.

Those who sow the wind, reap the whirling.

Thou art my GOD.

Three sixes are symbols of the anti-Christ.

Three types of haves: the haves, they have not, and they
haven't paid for it yet.

Threw it all, I've learned to depend on JESUS, threw it all.

Thy will be done.

Thy word is truth.

Time heals all wounds.

Time waits for no one.

Tithing is First Fruits.

Tithing is the gateway to prosperity.

To change your vibration, be grateful.

To concur, fear is the beginning of wisdom.

To forgive us is the pardon from GOD.

To his kingdom, there is no END.

Tomorrow isn't promised.

Tomorrow is the first day for the rest of your Life.

To PRAY shows your development with the LORD.

To see Evil and not speak on it, is Evil.

To some people, conscience is a poor memory of the soul.

To whom much is given, much is required.

Trials are sent to expose your weaknesses.

Trials must surrender to the triumphs.

Trouble is an asset.

Trouble is not chastisement.

Trouble is the gateway to discovering GOD.

Trouble is the womb of greatness.

Troubles that drive you to JESUS are a priceless treasure.

Troubles will help you find out who your real friends are.

Trouble transfers your noodle spine into steel.

Trouble will determine your friends.

Trust in the LORD with all your heart and soul.

Trust no one with your Life that you can't trust with your virtue too.

Truth always overrides the facts.

Truth be told.

Truth has a power all its own.

Truth, like beauty, is in the eye of the beholder.

Truth is the most important value that we have.

Truth without works is Death.

Turn loose what's in your hand and receive what GOD has for you in his hand.

Turn the other cheek.

Two kinds of Power: Power over people, or Power with people.

Two wrongs don't make a right.

"U"

Unconditional Love.
Unconfessed sin will destroy you.
Use it up, wear it out or do without.

"V"

Vengeance doesn't keep you warm at night.

Vengeance is mine sayeth the LORD.

Violence begets violence.

Violence is always the result of ignorance.

Virtue is its reward.

Vote the BIBLE.

"W"

Wages of sin are DEATH.

Walk away from sin to embrace the will of GOD.

Watch out for the third voice, it wants to be the only voice.

We are commanded by GOD, not by worry.

We are one generation from mocking GOD. (Stalin)

We are required to know when the 2nd coming of JESUS CHRIST is nearby. It's when the National Sunday Law passes.

We can't retract the decisions we've made, but we can attract the decisions we're going to make.

We come to the cross to represent CHRIST in the world.

We have been blessed by the father, in the Son, thru the Holy Spirit.

We have the right to choose the BIBLE way over the government's way.

We need balance in our Life.

We need to get back to the solid foundation of GOD.

We're all naked in the eyes of GOD.

We're now living in, "The Church Age".

We shall reap what we sow.

We walk by FAITH, not by sight.

We want what GOD has without being what GOD is, POWER.

We will know people in HEAVEN.

We will repeat the first (8) chapters of the book of ACTS.

What are you willing to die for?

What does believing in GOD really mean?

Whatever you need is in JESUS.

What prophets a man who gains the world but loses his soul.

What's important in Life is Life, not the result of Life.

What we think in our hearts, so are we.

What would it profit a man to inherit the world and lose his soul?

What you can walk away from, GOD can bring you too.

What you read and think about will take over you.

When a man lies with another man, like with a woman, it is an abomination.

When darkness falls, light will arise.

When GOD's about to change you, he will bring a person into your Life.

When GOD is in your Life, there's security.

When HELL freezes over.

When in doubt, do nothing.

When in doubt, tell the truth.

When Life gives you LEMONS, you make lemonade.

When setting out on a path of revenge, dig two graves.

When the DEVIL has a plan to take you out, GOD has a plan to keep you in.

When the righteous are in authority, people rejoice.

When the wicked are rulers, people morn.

When troubles grow, your character shows.

When trouble shows, your character grows.

When two think exactly alike, one is not needed.

When you are down to nothing, GOD's up to something.

When you become a child of GOD, he will defend you against your adversaries. When you bow to fear, you do not believe in GOD.

When you get bored, the enemy is setting you up for sin.

When you got a fish hooked, reel him in.

When you live by the BIBLE, it controls you.

When your conscience is saying to do something wrong and you know it's not right, that's SIN.

When you're down to nothing, GOD's up to something.

When you receive the HOLY SPIRIT, you speak the word of GOD boldly.

When you release what you have in your hand, GOD will release what's in his hand.

When you think you know more than GOD, that's ignorance going to seed.

Where there's a will, there's away.

Where there's Death, there will always be Death.

Where there's Life, there's hope.

Where there's thunder, there's lightning.

Where two are three are gathered in my name, I will be there.

Wherever your treasure is, is where your heart is.

Whoever shall take up the sword shall perish by the sword.

Will JESUS come back before 2023?

Winners don't quit, and quitters don't win.

Wisdom begins in wonder.

Wisdom comes with silence.

Wisdom is always an overmatch for Strength.

Wish big.

Witchcraft is never harmless.

Without FAITH, it's impossible the please GOD.

Without Jewish FAITH, there is no Christian FAITH.

Without Love you have nothing.

Worry is FAITH in fear.

Worry is interest paid on trouble before it happens.

Worry is like a treadmill, it wears you out and gets you nowhere.

Worry is practical atheism, not believing that GOD will take care of you.

Worry is sin.

Worry is something that you cannot have your own way, it shows, in reality, the distrust of GOD.

Worry is the mother of high blood pressure and cancer.

Worry makes cowards out of men.

Worry robs the body of sleep at night. Write the wrong.

Wrong came from the right, right didn't come from wrong.

Wrong follows wrong.

Wrong Life cannot be lived rightly.

"Y"

You are a child of GOD.

You are an original, don't die as a copy of someone else.

You are not born generous.

You aren't what you chose to be, you are what you and
GOD chose for you to be.

You can be religious and lost.

You can be what you want to be.

You can disagree without being disagreeable.

You can get what you want and not want what you get.

You can give without LOVING, but

you can't LOVE without giving.

You can judge a man by the tone of his voice.

You can never change what you will not confront.

You cannot achieve what you refuse to believe.

You cannot be removed from the foundation of your faith.

You can't change what you won't confront.

You cannot change yourself, you need the Holy Spirit.

You can't forgive totally with the handles up.

You can't follow a parked car.

You cannot have a positive life and a negative mind.

You cannot have resurrection without crucifixion.

You can't plant a roaming man's feet on the earth.

You can't run away from yourself, everywhere you go,
there you are.

You can't see the beauty outside yourself unless you can
see the beauty inside yourself. You can't serve GOD
and mammon both. (Mammon meaning money)

You can preach a better sermon with your life than with your lips.

You can trace all deterioration to a third voice.

You decide if you need a Miracle or not.

You do not break GOD's LAW, GOD's LAW will break you.

You don't choose your relatives.

You do not have to give in to temptations.

You don't read the BIBLE, it reads you.

You do what you do because you are what you are.

You have a friend in JESUS.

You have not because you asked not.

You have to believe it to receive it.

You have to be obedient to GOD's word.

You have to crawl before you walk.

You have to give, to receive.

You have to take the good with the bad.

You made your bed hard, so sleep in it.

You need a savior because you have a past you can't go back to.

You need supernatural powers because you have supernatural enemies.

You never have to convince GOD, he knows already.

Your arms are too short to box with GOD.

Your battlefield is your mind.

Your days are not promised but are numbered.

You reap what you sow.

Your feet are going to travel where you set your mind.

Your hair is so nappy, Wilson can't pick it.

Your mind will justify what your conscience condemns.

Your reward is not a thing, your reward is a KING.

Your speech has supernatural powers.

Your success for the rest of the week begins with Sunday's First Fruit.

You "re either a servant to JESUS or a slave to the serpent.

You're going to die, and you're going to be Judged.

You're here today and gone tomorrow.

You're judged by what you do when no one is watching.

You're not getting older, you're getting closer to the LORD.

You're not in the kingdom of GOD if you don't believe in the BIBLE.

You're only four (4) people away from meeting anybody in the world.

You're only young for a short while, but you've grown forever.

You're not ready to live until you are ready to die.

Your tongue is connected to your emotions.

You've succeeded in life when all you really want is only what you really need.

You were born to be blessed.

You will never possess what GOD has for you, until you believe in GOD.

You will never possess what you will not pursue.

You will not prosper until you believe that it's the LORD's will for you to prosper.

"Z"

ZACHARIAH 14, 12:2, 16:17

This is not the end of this book, I'll see you later.

THANKS!

www.ingramcontent.com/pod-product-compliance
Lightning Source LLC
Chambersburg PA
CBHW030305130626
46549CB00002B/700